☞ extremely im-
portant message
from the editors

please buy this publication

About
THE FIFTIES

by "The Usual Gang of Idiots"

LITTLE, BROWN AND COMPANY
Boston New York Toronto London

Also available:

 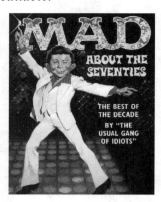

> Though Alfred E. Neuman wasn't the first to say "A fool and his money are soon parted," here's your chance to prove the old adage right—subscribe to *MAD*! Simply call 1-800-4-MADMAG and mention code 5BKC3. Operators are standing by (the water cooler).

MAD, BOY'S HEAD DEVICE, and all related indicia are trademarks of EC Publications, Inc.
Compilation and all new material copyright © 1997 by EC Publications, Inc.
All rights reserved.

No part of this book may be reproduced in any form or by any electronic or mechanical means, including information storage and retrieval systems, without permission in writing from the publisher, except by a reviewer, who may quote brief passages in a review.

FIRST EDITION

Library of Congress Cataloging-in-Publication Data

MAD about the fifties : the best of the decade / by "The usual gang of idiots."
    p. cm.
    ISBN 0-316-55808-7 (pbk.)
PN6728.M33M25   1997   97-4376
741.5'973 — dc21

10 9 8 7 6 5 4 3 2 1

RRD-OH

Published simultaneously in Canada by Little, Brown & Company (Canada) Limited
Printed in the United States of America

**This book is dedicated to the memory of Harvey Kurtzman,
the furshlugginer genius who started it all.**

—"The Usual Gang of Idiots"

Compiled and interior design by Grant Geissman

Special thanks to:
Charles Kochman (DC Comics),
Nick Meglin, John Ficarra, and Annie Gaines (*MAD* magazine),
Les Pockell and Monica Elias (BOMC),
Geoffrey Kloske (Little, Brown),
and especially "The Usual Gang of Idiots,"
those talented writers, artists, editors, and conspirators
who have rotted the minds of *MAD* readers for five decades.

FOREWORD

Early 1952: everyone was happy. EC Comics publisher Bill Gaines was happy because his small but solid line of comic books was not only highly regarded and influential, but also firmly in the black. Al Feldstein (an artist-writer-editor hyphenate) was happy to be turning out the lion's share of EC's output, including the very profitable horror comics (*Tales from the Crypt, Vault of Horror,* and *Haunt of Fear*) and the more creatively satisfying science fiction titles (*Weird Science* and *Weird Fantasy*). EC's stable of artists were happy, because the comic house provided them with a steady stream of good-paying work (at rates among the highest in the industry), with a check upon delivery—a rarity in the comics game. EC's rabid readers were happy, because they were convinced that what they were getting for their dimes was a cut above the average comic book, in terms of both artwork and story line.

Everyone was happy, that is, except Harvey Kurtzman (another artist-writer-editor hyphenate), who was running himself ragged researching, writing, laying out, drawing for, and editing the world's first true-to-life war comics, *Two-Fisted Tales* and *Frontline Combat.* Where Feldstein could write a story in a day (usually from a plot provided by Gaines), Kurtzman felt he couldn't write until he had all the background material together, a process that included talking to war veterans, reading historical accounts, going up on a test flight, and even sending assistant Jerry De Fuccio down in a submarine for a firsthand account. Every detail had to be accurate, right down to the buttons on uniforms. Needless to say, this process could (and did) take weeks. Kurtzman was producing work unsurpassed in the comic book field, then or now. The downside was that, for all the accolades, he simply wasn't making enough to support his family. He appealed to Gaines for a raise, but Gaines was caught in a conundrum. Feldstein was turning out seven books to Kurtzman's two, and payment was calculated by the number of books, not by the time it took to turn one out. Furthermore, although *Two-Fisted Tales* and *Frontline Combat* were the best books of their kind, they were only moderately profitable compared with EC's flagship horror titles. Gaines recognized that Kurtzman's work was first-rate, but he couldn't reconcile the quality/quantity equation.

The solution? If Harvey could sandwich in another book between the ones he was already doing (a book that could be done quickly, without all the heavy research), his income would go up by 50 percent. What kind of book might that be? Kurtzman was good with humor, so why not try that?

Nick Meglin: Harvey had a lot going for him. In addition to his . . .

What? Oh, it's you, Meglin. Not that I'm surprised by your intrusion. I just can't believe it took you so long.

N.M.: I feel like I'm in a rejected Back to the Future *movie script! First we did this in the* MAD About the Sixties *book, then the* Seventies, *and now the* Fifties? *Who are the geniuses behind this decade hopping?*

The same ones who suggested your constant interruptions for all these Forewords, I'm afraid.

N.M.: You mistake my colorful, informative, and insightful ornamentation to your long-winded historical ramblings for interruption? *Shmendrick! As I was saying, Harvey was more than a masterly visual talent—he had the ability to combine his literal narrative sense with a wonderful feel for whimsy and absurdity. An iconoclast (like most satirists), Harvey played his humor with subtlety and understatement rather than heavy-handed cynicism.*

I couldn't agree more.

N.M.: An old trick, G.G. By agreeing with me, you think you can now take the credit for my profound, meaningful revelations. Well, it won't work! Now get back to your meaningless drivel!

What a kidder!

Thus, out of a simple (yet pressing) need for more income, *MAD*, a publication destined to become an American institution, was born.

The actual attendees present at *MAD*'s birth are in disagreement. All concerned agree upon the reason *MAD* was created, but the facts beyond that vary depending on whose camp you're in. Bill Gaines always maintained that it was he who proposed that the new magazine be humorous, since the first material in Kurtzman's portfolio that Gaines saw (and that got him hired at EC) were the comedic and surreal *Hey Look!* pages Harvey had done for Stan Lee's Timely/Marvel Comics in the late 1940s. Kurtzman, on the other hand, insisted that *he* proposed a humor book, since humor continuities were something he had done before and enjoyed. Also open to debate is who actually coined the title "*MAD*." Harvey maintained that it was his title and his alone, but Gaines and Feldstein lay claim to having suggested calling the publication "EC's MAD Mag," which was a phrase the Crypt Keeper often used in the EC horror comics. According to Feldstein, Kurtzman volleyed back with, "Well, *MAD* sounds better than 'EC's MAD Mag.'" "And that," says Feldstein, "was *it*."

from *Weird Fantasy* #15, September–October, 1952

EC "house ad" for MAD #1; the figure in the Napoleon hat is Bill Gaines.

Feldstein also recalls there being a kind of friendly competition around the EC offices, with the editors trying to outdo each other, and sometimes even pitching ideas around for one another's separate projects. It was in this spirit that another EC artist-writer-editor, Johnny Craig, contributed the comic book's early subtitle: "Humor in a Jugular Vein." Beyond this, the "real" story of *MAD*'s origin will probably never be untangled. As Kurtzman himself once remarked about *MAD*'s beginnings (quoting an old adage), "Success has many fathers, while failure is an orphan." At the end of the day, however, how the book came to be, and even who came up with the title, is of little importance, for the creative genius behind all the material in the early *MAD* was Harvey Kurtzman. And about that there is no dispute.

The first issue of *MAD*, a 10¢ comic book, was cover-dated Oct.-Nov., 1952, and appeared on the nation's newsstands several months before that. The initial concept was to satirize the kind of stories that EC had been turning out: horror, science fiction, crime, and even the recently deceased romance comics. The artists selected for *MAD* were simply the same core group of artists who had been working on Kurtzman's war books: Bill Elder, John Severin, Jack Davis, and Wallace Wood. The stories, while comedic, were nonetheless aimed at an older, more sophisticated reader than was the average "funny book."

N.M.: Harvey, whose own strong and highly visual narrative talent could be likened to that of a film director, knew these artist's strengths and played into them, casting each in roles they would be most comfortable in. Thus Wood, an aficionado of Hal Foster's Prince Valiant *and Alex Raymond's* Flash Gordon, *was selected to illustrate their satirical counterparts. Elder, who could create absurdly maniacal characters, got to originate "The Mole" and portray* The Shadow *in ways that would define them in the minds of many of us forever. As for* The Lone Ranger, *who better than Jack Davis, the fastest drawer of the West? And the African jungle has never been the same since Severin's "Melvin of the Apes," swinging from vines, earned frequent flyer miles the hard way.*

As Kurtzman struggled through *MAD*'s birth pangs, Gaines was facing another kind of struggle. Comic book industry pundits thought Gaines was crazy to invest money in what was quite obviously a losing proposition. Comic books, they said, appealed to children, not adults. In a 1954 *Writer's Digest* article, Bill Gaines wrote: "So they were right. *MAD* #1 lost money. My editor, Harvey Kurtzman, looked at me mournfully. I looked at him mournfully. *MAD* #2 lost money. *MAD* #3 lost money. *MAD* #4 lost money. Kurtzman and I were not looking at each other at all when the sales reports began to come in on *MAD* #5. With a bang, we had done it!" Convinced Kurtzman was on to something, Gaines had carried the book at a loss until it found its audience—another rarity in comics. While *MAD* #4 may have lost money, it contained the fledgling publication's first bona fide classic— "Superduperman." *MAD* had found its voice, satirizing not just generic comic book *styles*, but specific comic book and comic strip features. And Kurtzman didn't stop there: he began taking on movies, television, politics, and various other aspects of popular culture. The pundits were proved wrong: the comic book *MAD was* a hit, even spawning a host of mediocre (and short-lived) imitations. And for a time, everyone was happy.

Fast-forward to 1955. *MAD* had been a comic book for nearly three years. For all of *MAD*'s success, Kurtzman was still not satisfied. As brilliant as the work was, Harvey still felt he was slumming in the world of comics, and he longed to break into the world of magazines, or "slicks," as they were known in the trade. Kurtzman had been entertaining a job offer from *Pageant,* and he told Gaines he was thinking of leaving. To keep Kurtzman in the fold, Gaines offered to let him re-invent *MAD* as a 25¢ slick, an offer Harvey readily accepted. As Kurtzman told *MAD* writer Frank Jacobs in *The MAD World of William M. Gaines:* "The next day was one of the most exciting times in my life. I ran down to the newsstand and bought a bunch of slick magazines to see what other people were doing. I was scared to death when we abandoned the comic format, and I couldn't sleep wondering whether *MAD* would succeed in its new format." He needn't have worried. The first magazine issue (#24, July, 1955) flew off the newsstands, prompting a second printing, which is all but unheard-of in magazine publishing. Kurtzman, who had written virtually all the material in the comic book *MAD*, instituted a more open-door policy. Among the new contributing writers: writer/artist Al Jaffee (a friend from their days at New York's High School of Music and Art), Bernard Shir-Cliff, and Phil Interlandi (another writer/artist). Celebrities who were enamored of the publication and stepped up to join the fun included Roger Price, Stan Freberg, Jules Feiffer, and Ernie Kovacs, among others.

Despite the happy buzz surrounding the new *MAD*, there were still some problems. Officially a bimonthly, the time between issues was often much longer; in spite of the additional writers and artists, the perfectionist Kurtzman just could not stay on top of his deadlines. And he was demanding more money—not for himself, but to spend on the magazine. But it was money Gaines couldn't afford. Harvey's deadline problems and demands did not endear him to *MAD*'s publisher. The Gaines/Kurtzman relationship, which had been quite friendly, became increasingly strained.

After producing five issues of the magazine, Harvey found that he had a not-so-secret admirer in the young Hugh Hefner, who had recently launched *Playboy*—the other great success story of 1950s magazine publishing. Hefner and Kurtzman met, and found themselves to be on the same wavelength. With Hefner waiting in the wings, Kurtzman went to Gaines and demanded 51 percent ownership of *MAD*, a demand Kurtzman almost certainly knew Gaines would not meet. "I wanted control of the editorial package," Harvey told Frank Jacobs. "I didn't have it really. Bill gave me the freedom to write what I wanted, but there were larger questions, like the design of the magazine and how much I could spend on it. I had no power in this area." Predictably, Gaines refused, and Kurtzman made his exit. Kurtzman and Hefner almost immediately began work on a lush, expensively produced new humor magazine called *Trump*. Gaines was distraught, convinced that without Kurtzman there could be no *MAD*. Adding insult to injury was the fact that Kurtzman had taken with him most of *MAD*'s artists, with the exception of Wallace Wood, who remained loyal to Gaines. (For a short while, Wood actually worked for both *Trump* and *MAD*, until a "with us or against us" ultimatum from Hefner and Kurtzman caused Wood to choose to stick with *MAD*.)

On the advice of close friend (and fellow publisher) Lyle Stuart, Bill brought in former EC stalwart Al Feldstein (who had been let go after the collapse of Gaines's comic book empire) to take over as *MAD*'s editor. Kurtzman's former assistant, Jerry De Fuccio, stayed on and helped write some early articles.

N.M.: *Jerry had done prose filler pages (some humorous, some straight) for many of the EC Comics, in addition to working as Kurtzman's assistant. He had a degree in English literature, and as a writer was qualified well beyond what was required of him in comics. But he had an enormous devotion to the medium and was delighted to be a part of it, in any capacity. He was a kind and generous friend to all of us.*

Nick Meglin, who had sold some ideas to *Panic*, was the first new hire. Hey, Nick, were those guys desperate, or what?

N.M.: *Obviously, they were* beyond *desperate!* Panic *was EC's own entry into the flood of* MAD *knockoffs that surfaced. "If everyone else is doing it, why not us?" countered Gaines. When he took over* MAD *magazine, Feldstein called and asked me to try my hand at articles, which I did to help pay expenses as I peddled my illustration samples in a futile quest to become a professional book illustrator. When* MAD *offered me the security of a full-time job as an associate editor, I took it, believing the job to be a short-term stay until the Army drafted me for a two-year hitch. I sold a bunch of* MAD *articles while defending our nation.*

Lucky for us we weren't engaged in any wars at the time!

N.M.: Even luckier I didn't start any! When MAD *asked me to come back full-time after my discharge, I agreed immediately. My daughter had been born, and I wasn't ready to face the freelance world in any capacity just yet. I figured it would be just a short-term, temporary stay. That was forty years ago.*

Some "short-term, temporary stay"!

Art director John Putnam also stayed (with production man Lenny "The Beard" Brenner joining him at the end of 1958), and the small staff began to pick up the pieces. "I don't know how the first few issues got done," Feldstein has said, "but they got done. It was just one incident of serendipity after another. All these talented people were walking into the office, not aware that there'd been this terrible change—that Harvey had left and taken all the artists with him. I don't think they knew that there was a new editor who was on his knees praying for artists and writers to help him do his job." Artists answering his prayers: Don Martin, George Woodbridge, Mort Drucker, Norman Mingo, Kelly Freas, Bob Clarke, and Dave Berg (with EC veterans Wallace Wood and Joe Orlando also contributing). The first new writer in the door was Frank Jacobs, followed by Paul Laikin, Tom Koch, and Gary Belkin. They were joined a few years later by Larry Siegel and the returning Al Jaffee. Interestingly, both had come to *MAD* after working with Kurtzman on the worthy but ill-fated *Trump* and *Humbug*. Other noteworthy writers contributing (squeaking in just as the decade was ending) were Arnie Kogen, Sy Reit, and Donald Reilly.

Feldstein, who was nothing if not a pragmatist, got the magazine back on track and back on deadline. With a regular schedule and what was arguably a more accessible package, circulation began to increase. By the end of 1958, *MAD* would boast a million copies sold per issue.

Soon after Feldstein's arrival at *MAD*, the impishly grinning "What—me worry?" face and the name "Alfred E. Neuman" were wedded once and for all, and Alfred became the magazine's cover boy and mascot. It was Harvey Kurtzman who found the face, and appropriated it for the cover of the first *MAD* paperback book, *The MAD Reader* (published in 1954 by Ballantine Books).

Kurtzman began to sprinkle "the face" around the magazine under various names, and he appealed to the readership in the letter columns for information leading to the original source of the image. The "first" appearance of the face could not be located then or now, but it's been determined that it dates back to at least the turn of the century and had been used to advertise everything from "painless dentistry" to 1940s anti-President Roosevelt sentiments.

After Kurtzman's departure, Feldstein had the image fleshed out in full color by illustrator Norman Mingo; Mingo's Alfred ran for President on the cover of issue #30 (December, 1956), and appeared enshrined on Mount Rushmore on the cover of the following issue. Nick Meglin, in particular, lobbied Gaines and Feldstein to permanently adopt their newly found cover icon, and Alfred has graced the cover of virtually every issue since. Mingo's quintessential rendering of Alfred became the model from which all other versions would be fashioned.

Letters page, MAD #26, November, 1955

N.M.: *A want ad in the* New York Times *for a serious illustrator attracted advertising illustrator and former* Saturday Evening Post *artist Norman Mingo. This well-dressed, distin-*

guished-looking gentleman (who sported a white moustache and matching Van Dyke beard), appeared to be the antithesis of the MAD *sensibility. Mingo's eight 1950s-era covers (on issues #30 to #37), however, provided two important ingredients: an immediately likable and recognizable cover icon, coupled with Mingo's classy and classic rendering style (a style that was a marked contrast to* MAD*'s self-effacing attitude—that* MAD *produced "garbage"). After Mingo's departure (he wouldn't return until the end of 1962), science fiction illustrator Kelly Freas took over as* MAD*'s cover artist for virtually the rest of the 1950s; his elfin and whimsical images of Alfred were equally well-loved by readers.*

MAD exploded like a bottle rocket in the midst of the button-down, Eisenhower 1950s. While there had been joke books and humorous burlesque magazines, there had been nothing quite like MAD. In an era rife with Cold War paranoia (and under the shadow of the not-so-distant explosion of the atomic bomb that ended World War II), MAD was a jolt of insanity that, paradoxically, could be felt to be more sane than the "real" world it was harpooning.

MELVIN COZNOWSKI

Because MAD was begun by Harvey Kurtzman, a brilliant satirist (but a poor businessman), there developed what came to be known as the "Kurtzman Cult," a group of aficionados wildly devoted to Kurtzman's MAD, and for whom the later Feldstein-edited version was entirely unpalatable. In truth, while Kurtzman more than pointed the way, many of the features and artists that are now so indelibly identified with MAD were developed under Feldstein's editorship. Indeed, many of what have become MAD's most popular features (including Berg's "Lighter Side," Jaffee's "Fold-Ins," Drucker's movie parody caricatures, Sergio Aragonés's "marginals," and Prohias's "SPY vs SPY") were not so much as a gleam in their creator's eyes in the 1950s—these features didn't even begin to appear until the early 1960s, years after Kurtzman abandoned ship.

MEL HANEY
"What, me worry?"

Some historians float the theory that if Harvey Kurtzman had stayed on, MAD might have developed only a cult following—hailed as innovative and groundbreaking, but never evolving into the American pop cultural icon that it is today. We can never know, but what we *can* say is that for millions of people, the world would not be the same if their minds hadn't been rotted by MAD, in either its comic book or magazine

incarnation. Kurtzman's *MAD*, for example, planted the seeds of anarchy in such future sixties underground comix cartoonists as Robert Crumb, Gilbert Shelton, Bill Griffith, and Rick Griffin, as well as in future "Monty Python" member/visionary film director Terry Gilliam. In fact, because of his profound influence, Kurtzman came to be regarded as the father of the underground comix movement. Kurtzman, ever modest, demanded a "blood test."

The Feldstein-edited version of *MAD* has had an equally profound effect upon its readership as an indispensable rite of passage, a kind of primer into the ways of the world. Indeed, for all but the oldest of the Baby Boomers (that now-graying but eternally Peter Pan segment of the population), there has always been *MAD* (in one form or another), just as there has always been television, Walt Disney, and rock 'n' roll.

N.M.: *Enough already! Your version of MAD's fifties history has taken longer than our actually living it! To think we may have to do this again if our publisher believes a MAD About the Eighties collection is in order. Or out of order, judging by the sequence of this series so far!*

HOOHAH!

—Grant Geissman, who, continuing with tradition,
was interrupted yet again by Nick Meglin

GRANT GEISSMAN is the author of *Collectibly MAD* (Kitchen Sink Press), the history of *MAD* as shown by its own collectibles, and the compiler/annotator of *MAD About the Sixties*, *MAD About the Seventies* (Little, Brown and Company) and *MAD Grooves* (Rhino), a collection of the best from the *MAD* record albums. In his spare time, he is an in-demand session guitarist who has recorded with such artists as Quincy Jones, Paula Abdul, Chuck Mangione, Van Dyke Parks, and Brian Wilson.

1952-1955

Fall, 1952: General Dwight D. Eisenhower and his running mate, Richard Nixon, are gearing up for November's presidential election; they will defeat the Adlai Stevenson/John Sparkman ticket by a landslide. Among the Top Ten-rated TV shows are *I Love Lucy*, *Arthur Godfrey's Talent Scouts*, *Dragnet*, and *You Bet Your Life* (starring Groucho Marx). One third of the homes in America have TV sets. Among the top-rated movie stars: Dean Martin and Jerry Lewis, Gary Cooper, Bing Crosby, Bob Hope, John Wayne, Jimmy Stewart, and Doris Day. General Motors announced in July that, for the first time, air conditioning would be offered as an option on some of its car models. And a new comic book has appeared on the nation's crowded newsstands: *MAD*.

The first issue of *MAD* (Oct.-Nov., 1952) consisted of Harvey Kurtzman's parodies of EC's own comic book line. Kurtzman's "slithering blob" cover was a swipe at the often gruesome EC horror comics, which Kurtzman disliked. Paradoxically, it was EC's highly profitable horror comics that permitted the birth and extended underwriting of an untested project like *MAD*. Also appearing on this cover is *MAD*'s first use of the proper noun "Melvin" (a name made famous by Martin and Lewis), which Kurtzman would use again and again in his parodies.

The Kurtzman-illustrated covers to issues #2 and #3 are further riffs on EC's horror comics. The Bill Elder "private eye" cover to issue #5 is the only front cover art Elder did for *MAD*; as was customary, however, Kurtzman probably provided a detailed rough guide of the cover for Elder to follow.

Many of the comic book *MAD*'s covers were tied in to an interior feature. Covers that relate to stories contained in this compilation include #6 ("Ping Pong!") and #7 ("Shermlock Shomes!").

The Basil Wolverton-illustrated cover to *MAD* #11 (May, 1954), coupled with the "Beware of Imitations!" ad containing an actual *Life* magazine cover (appearing later in this section) caused *Life* to seriously threaten legal action. To diffuse the situation, *MAD* publisher Bill Gaines had to send a letter promising not to do it again. Although Basil Wolverton only did a handful of pieces for *MAD*, his unique "spaghetti and meatball" style of illustration was perfectly suited to the publication. Kurtzman had long been aware of Wolverton's art; they had appeared together in the pages of Stan Lee's teenage comics of the late 1940s. *MAD* trivia: the photo background of the New York skyline on the cover was shot by Kurtzman out of the window of the men's room of EC's downtown office building at 225 Lafayette Street.

The cover to issue #14 (August, 1954) features Kurtzman's airbrushed retouching of Leonardo Da Vinci's *Mona Lisa*, which got *MAD* in hot water yet again. "The things we got into the most trouble with were the things that we never dreamed would get us into trouble," Bill Gaines told comics historian John Benson in 1973. "Like when we had the Mona Lisa on the cover," continued Gaines, "and the Catholics thought it was the Virgin Mary." Another such example was the "composition book" cover of issue #20 (February, 1955), which the highly regarded *Hartford Courant* newspaper editorially blasted for actually encouraging kids to sneak the comic book into class.

The "connect the dot" cover to *MAD* #18 (December, 1954), with dots connected, spells out "can't draw very well can you." This cover has created a latter-day problem for serious collectors: it is hard to find copies of the issue whose dots have not been connected by the book's original owners.

The cover to issue #21 (March, 1955) is a parody of the Johnson Smith and Co. ads that regularly appeared in comic books and magazines of the time. "Every sentence is funny," Kurtzman told John Benson. "About a year's worth of writing went into that cover. It's sort of like reading The Lord's Prayer on the head of a pin." Hopefully, at least some of the material will be legible at the reduced size the cover appears in this book. Johnson Smith, incidently, is still in business, selling "things you never knew existed!" Completing the circle, the company has recently offered some of the *MAD* reprint compilation books.

"Mole!," from *MAD* #2 (December 1952-January 1953), is a bizarre little story that gives a good idea of the material in *MAD*'s first few issues, before Kurtzman hit upon the notion of specific parodies. The character of the Mole was an invention of Bill Elder's that was fleshed out into a full comic book continuity by Kurtzman. Although Kurtzman quickly abandoned this type of material, Melvin Mole's "dig, dig, dig!" litany is fondly remembered by *MAD*'s early readership.

The "Lone Stranger!" story (from *MAD* #3, February-March 1953), illustrated by Jack Davis, was *MAD*'s first direct parody of a TV show. The long-running *Lone Ranger* series began life on the radio in 1933, and was brought to television in 1949 by the ABC Network. The show proved to be one of ABC's greatest early success stories, running until 1957. Clayton Moore starred as The Lone Ranger, and Jay Silverheels appeared as The Lone Ranger's faithful sidekick, Tonto (parodied here as "Pronto"). Memorable catchphrases from the series were "Who was that masked man?" and "Hi ho Silver, away!," both of which were deftly dispatched by Kurtzman's poison pen.

The parody of DC Comics' most enduring character, "Superduperman!" (*MAD* #4, April-May 1953, illustrated by Wallace Wood), is, as discussed in the foreword, *MAD*'s first bona fide classic. In this story, Wood took Bill Elder's "side gags on the walls" device (first used in the "Mole!") to a new level; there are so many of these gags in "Superduperman" that one has to give it several readings to catch them all without losing the thread of the story. Kurtzman's lampoon is a comment on the then-ongoing lawsuit DC had filed against Fawcett's *Captain Marvel*, which DC claimed flagrantly violated its *Superman* copyright. Although Superman was the first costumed comic book super hero, he certainly wasn't the last, and at the time of the suit the *Captain Marvel* family of comic books were the bigger sellers. "Superduperman!" was a first on another front: it was the first *MAD* story to cause the threat of legal action. The head muckety-mucks at DC Comics were not at all amused by the spoof, and to avoid legal action Gaines gave the first in a long line of promises not to do it again (promises that would be broken by subsequent *MAD* articles, sooner or later). *MAD* didn't do a takeoff on *Superman* again for quite a while, but with issue #8 (December 1953-January 1954), Kurtzman and Wood took on DC's second best-known character in "Bat Boy and Rubin!" The "Notice! This story is a lampoon!" lettering posted in the splash panel was put in specifically for DC's lawyers, in case they again got the wrong idea about *MAD*'s intent. Ironically, a Byzantine series of ownership changes has caused *MAD*, lo these many years later, to now be published under DC's aegis, as is Captain Marvel.

"Melvin of the Apes!" (#6, August-September 1953, illustrated by John Severin) lampoons Edgar Rice Burroughs's venerable creation, *Tarzan*. This was actually the second time Kurtzman and Severin had visited the Tarzan character; in issue #2 they tackled the subject in a story called "Melvin!" Kurtzman occasionally did this; if he thought a subject was worthy of revisiting, he had no compunction against returning to the scene of the crime. "Shermlock Shomes!" (from #7, October-November 1953, illustrated by Bill Elder) was also revisited in a later issue, as was "The Lone Stranger!"

"Ping Pong!" (#6, August-September 1953), illustrated by Bill Elder, is a spoof of the classic 1933 RKO Pictures spectacular, *King Kong*. The then twenty-year-old film may have been in re-release at the time of *MAD*'s version, prompting the parody; in any case, *King Kong* was ingrained enough in the pop culture consciousness to spoof, even if it was not a "contemporary" film. Kurtzman's twist at the story's end is, as *MAD*'s readers had come to expect, an inspired one.

For "The Raven," Kurtzman simply gave the Edgar Allan Poe poem to Bill Elder, and told him to have his way with it—a job Elder clearly approached with relish. This was likely the first exposure to the Poe classic for many of *MAD*'s fans. Few readers of *MAD*'s "The Raven" are able to go back and read the original poem without thinking of the Elder version.

"Starchie" is Kurtzman's look at the popular and long-running *Archie*, illustrated by Bill Elder (#12, June 1954). Kurtzman's approach to the story is to make the "typical teenage" characters not so typical. Elder's background signage is, yet again, worth a separate sweep through the story.

"Mickey Rodent!" (illustrated by Bill Elder, #19, January, 1955) takes a long, hard look at Walt Disney's various characters. Elder's background signs again enrich the story, although in this case it is a little hard to tell where Elder begins and Kurtzman leaves off; signs that specifically advance the story are likely Kurtzman's, and the rest are probably Elder's. Elder here reveals himself to be a master craftsman; his aping of the Disney "house style" is flawless. As the story progresses, "Darnold" begins to smell a rat. Elder's dramatic use of underlighting in the penultimate panel sets up a tension that propels the reader to the story's climax, where Disney's entire anthropomorphic mythology is deconstructed—in one panel, yet!

"Howdy Dooit!" (#18, December, 1954) was originally presented in black and white, except for the very first panel. Even though comic books were virtually always printed in full color, Kurtzman employed the use of black and white to better simulate the black and white pictures then commonly seen on America's TV screens. (While some shows were being broadcast in color at the time, having a color TV set at home did not become commonplace until the late 1960s.) *Howdy Doody* was an enormously popular children's show, running each weekday for thirteen years (1947-1960), and spawning a host of merchandising tie-ins: comic books, records, games, clothing, dolls, and more. *Howdy*'s creator, Buffalo Bob Smith, was born in Buffalo, New York, in 1917. The role of Clarabell the clown was originated by Robert Keeshan, who left in 1955 to create (and star in) another venerable children's show, *Captain Kangaroo*.

Ending this section is "Flesh Garden!" (#11, May, 1954), illustrated by Wallace Wood. Wood had been a great admirer of the *Flash Gordon* comic strip and the artwork of its creator, Alex Raymond, so Wood no doubt savored the opportunity to pay satirical homage to one of his idols. Wood's artwork on "Flesh Garden!" looks to have been influenced by the *Flash Gordon* movie serials as well; "Flesh" bears a strong resemblance to Buster Crabbe, who played Flash in these serials.

It is as good a time as any to note that while there was no overt sex in the twenty-three issues of the *MAD* comic book, there were very generous helpings of sexy and scantily clad women, which for the most part were rendered by Wallace Wood. (Elder's women also could be sexy, but not to the extent that Wood's women were.) To impressionable young minds in the repressed and buttoned-down 1950s, this form of titillation was better than nothing.

Unlike "Howdy Dooit!," "Flesh Garden!" was originally printed in full comic book color. Printing the story in black and white in this book (and on much nicer paper than the cheap pulp used in the comics) gives us the opportunity to view Wood's exquisitely rendered figures as they were originally drawn.

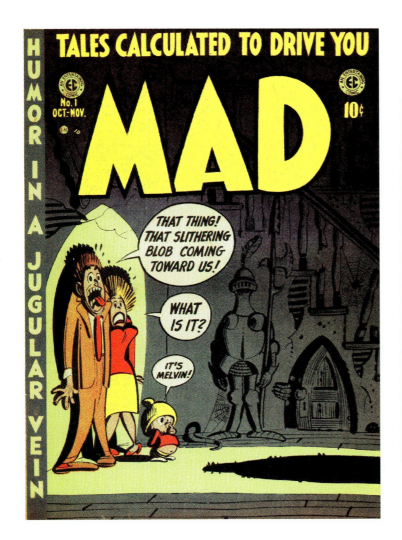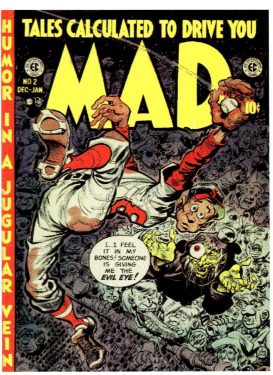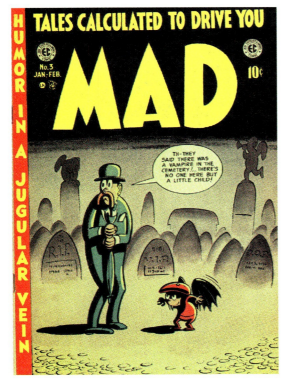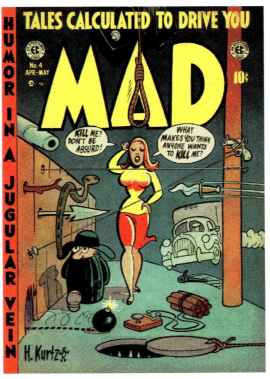

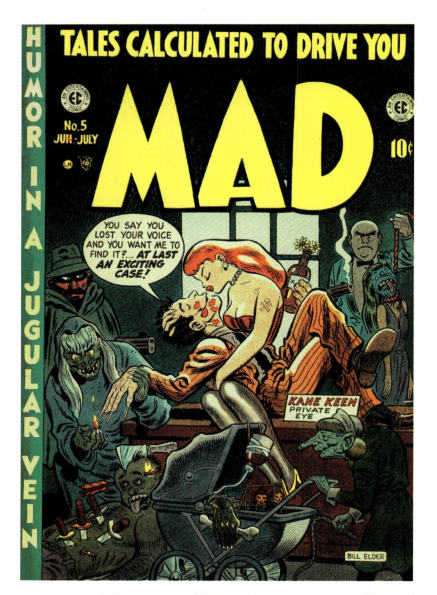
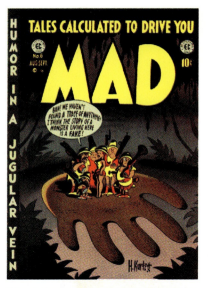
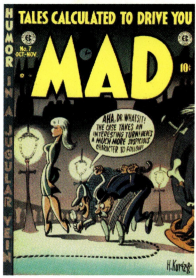

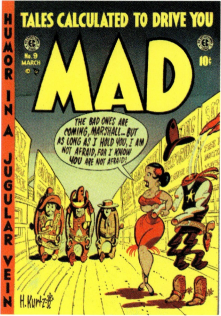

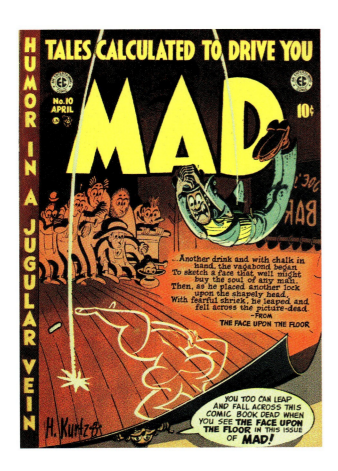
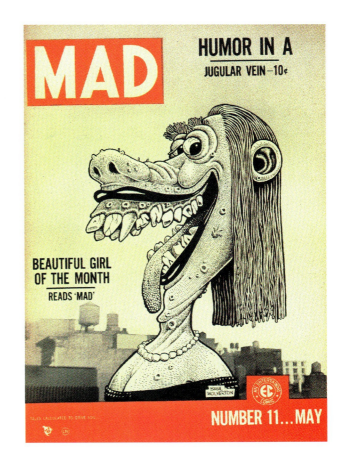

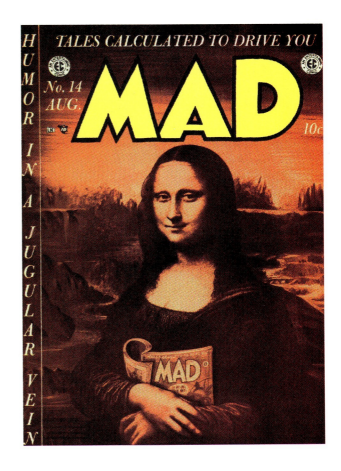

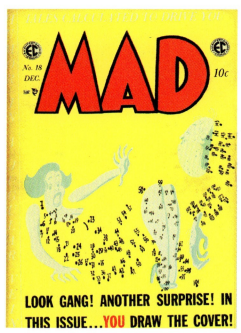
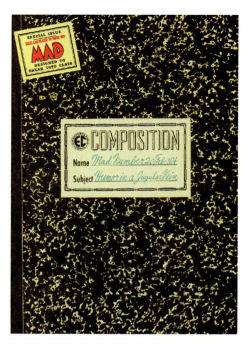
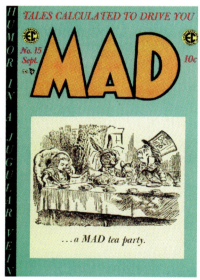
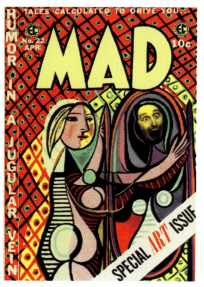

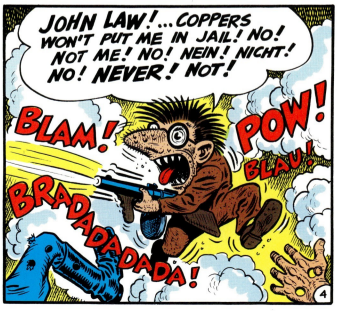

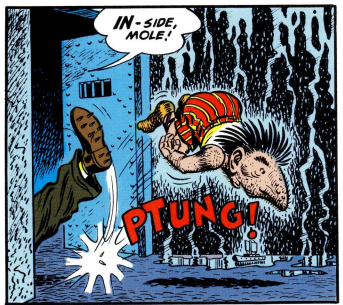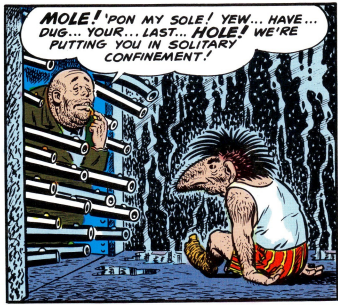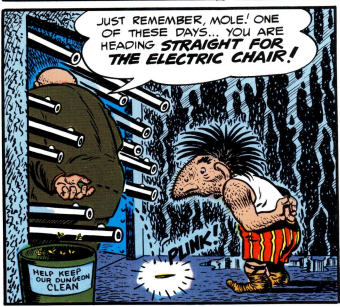

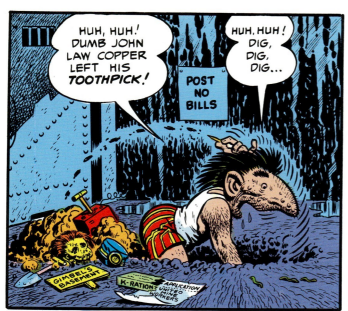

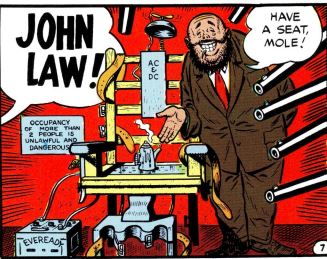

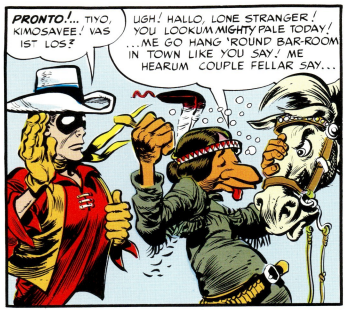

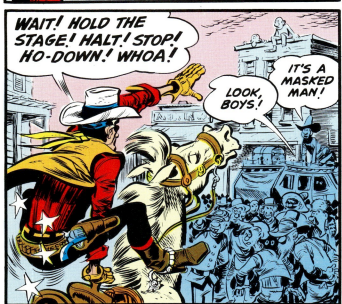

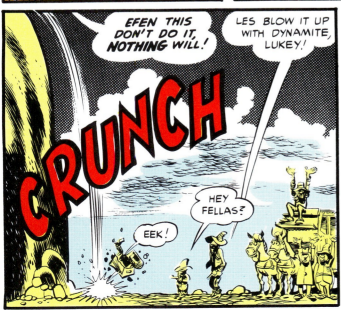

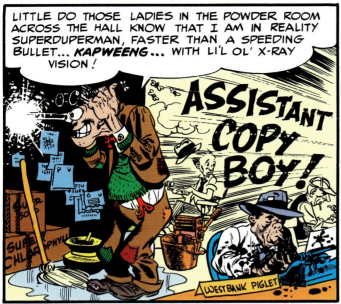

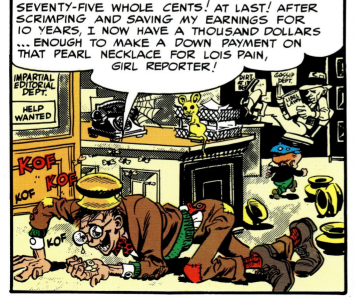
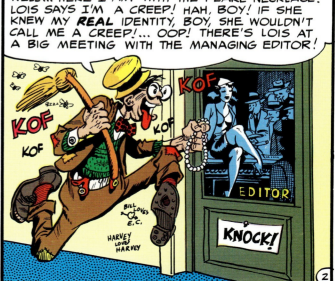

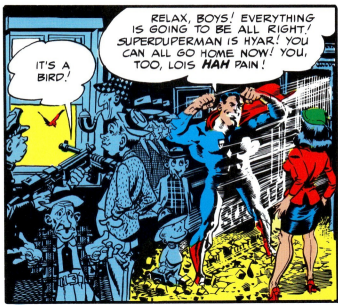

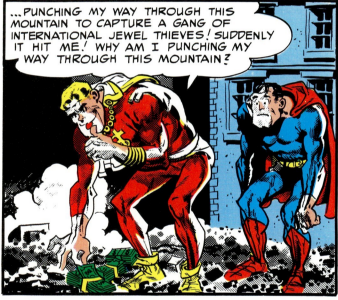
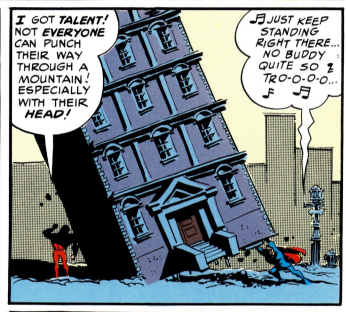

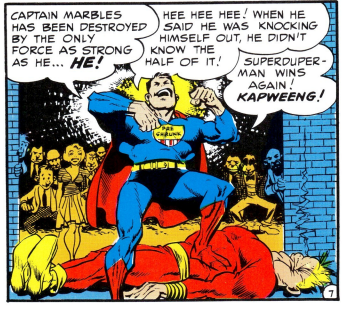

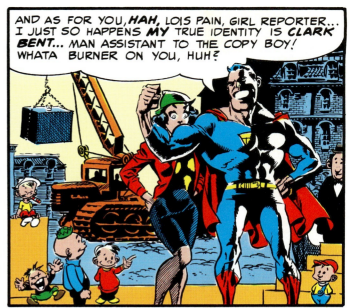

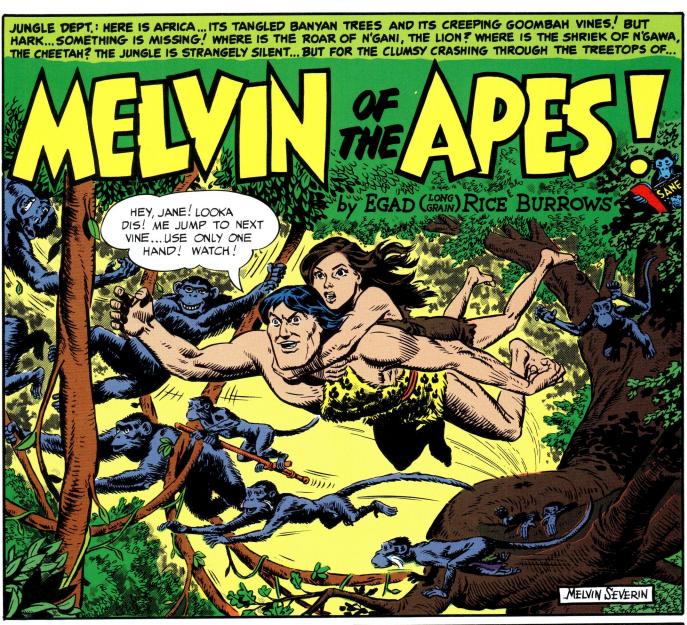

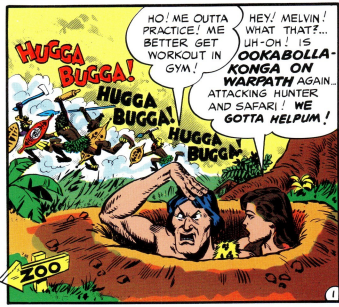

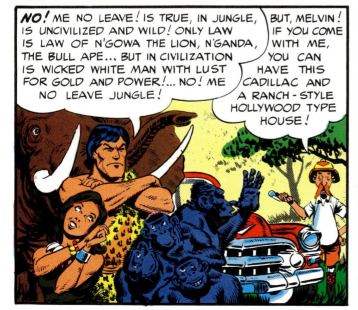

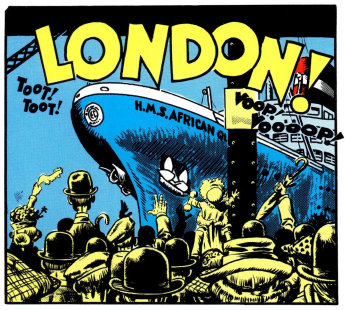

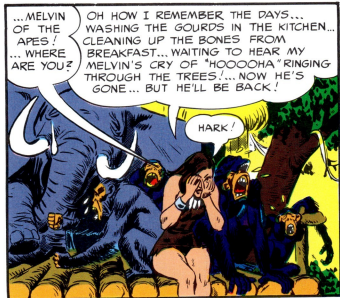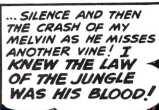

HORROR DEPT.: THE TALE WAS TOLD BY AN OLD SEA-FARING MAN, BABBLING IN DELIRIUM BEFORE HE DIED! BABBLING AMONGST THE FLOTSAM AND JETSAM TOSSED UPON THE CONEY ISLAND SHORE HE BABBLED... ABOUT A MYSTERIOUS ISLAND IN THE TROPICS... ABOUT THE LOST TRIBE OF THE OOKABOLAPONGA... ABOUT THEIR GOD...

PING PONG!

THE TROPICS!... SOMEWHERE IN THE LATITUDES, SOUTH OF THE SARGOSSA SEA, A PEA-SOUP FOG... SO THICK YOU COULD CUT IT WITH A KNIFE... HUGS THE OCEAN!

AND INSIDE THE FOG... A SHIP RIDES LIKE A GHOST... A BLACK SHIP WITH A GRIM-FACED FEARLESS CREW OF MEN... RIDING TO ITS DESTINY... WITH **DEATH**...WITH **PONG**!

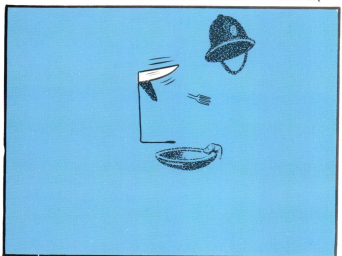

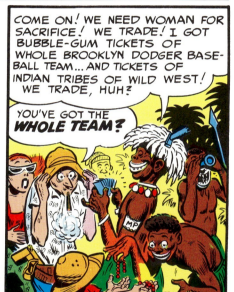

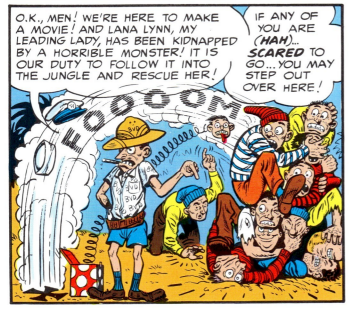

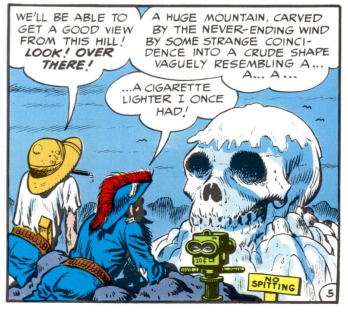

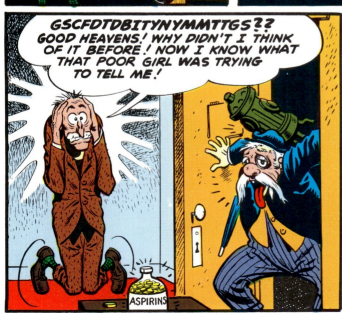

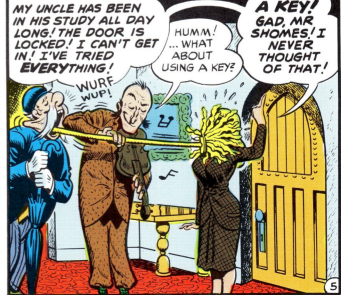

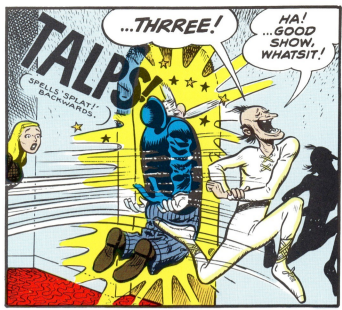

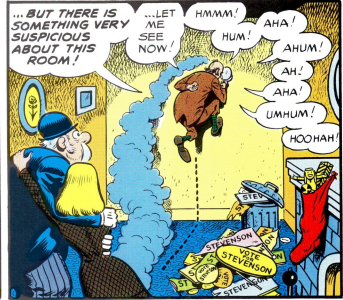

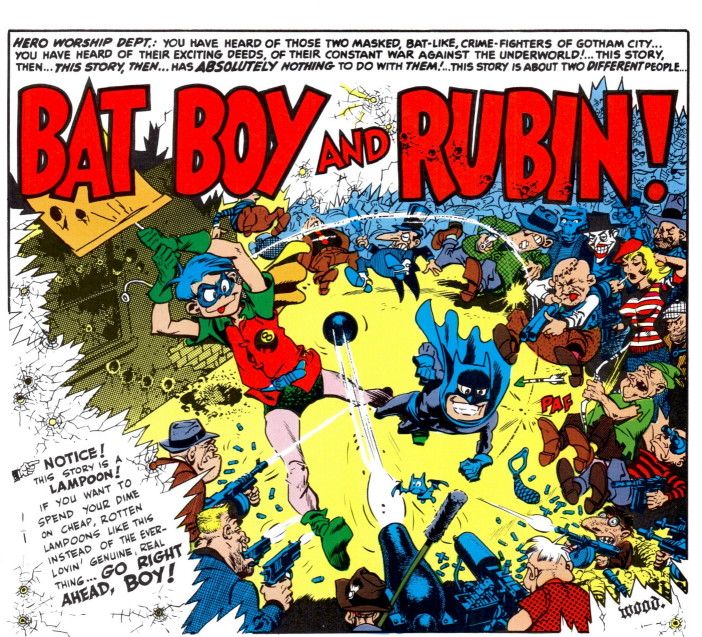

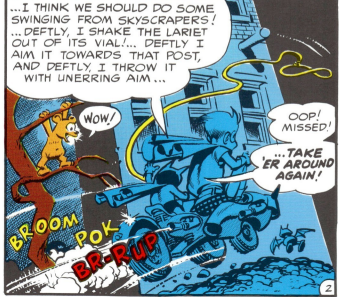

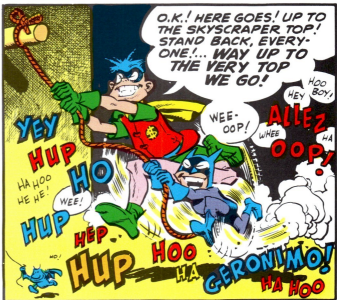

And the silken, sad, uncertain rustling of each purple curtain
Thrilled me - filled me with fantastic terrors never felt before;
So that now, to still the beating of my heart, I stood repeating

"'Tis some visiter entreating entrance at my chamber door—
Some late visiter entreating entrance at my chamber door;—
This it is and nothing more."

Presently my soul grew stronger; hesitating then no longer,
"Sir," said I, "or Madam, truly your forgiveness I implore;

But the fact is I was napping and so gently you came rapping,
And so faintly you came tapping, tapping at my chamber door,

That I scarce was sure I heard you"— here I opened wide the door;—

Darkness there and nothing more.

Deep into that darkness peering, long I stood there wondering, fearing
Doubting, dreaming dreams no mortal ever dared to dream before;
But the silence was unbroken, and the stillness gave no token,

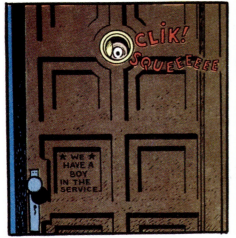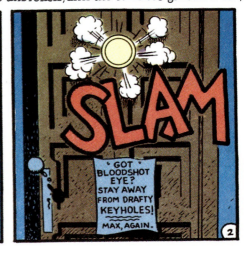

And the only word there spoken was the whispered word, "Lenore?"
This I whispered, and an echo murmured back the word, "Lenore!"
    Merely this and nothing more.

Let me see, then, what thereat is, and this mystery explore —
Let my heart be still a moment and this mystery explore;—
    'Tis the wind and nothing more!"

But, with mien of lord or lady, perched above my chamber door—
Perched upon a bust of Pallas just **above** my chamber door—
    Perched, and sat, and nothing more.

Back into the chamber turning, all my soul within me burning,
Soon again I heard a tapping somewhat louder than before.
"Surely, said I, "surely that is something at my window
        lattice;

Open here I flung the shutter, when, with many a flirt and flutter,
In there stepped a stately Raven of the saintly days of yore;
Not the least obeisance made he; not a minute stopped
        or stayed he;

Then this ebony bird beguiling my sad fancy into
        smiling,
By the grave and stern decorum of the countenance
        it wore,

"Though thy crest be shorn and shaven, thou," I said,
   "art sure no craven,
Ghastly grim and ancient Raven wandering from
   the Nightly shore—

Tell me what thy lordly name is on the Night's
   Plutonian shore!"

   Quoth the Raven "Nevermore."

Much I marvelled this ungainly fowl to hear
   discourse so plainly,
Though its answer little meaning—little relevancy bore;
For we cannot help agreeing that no living human being

Ever yet was blessed with seeing bird above his chamber door—
Bird or beast upon the sculptured bust above his chamber door,

   With such name as "Nevermore."

But the Raven, sitting lonely on the placid bust, spoke only
That one word, as if his soul in that one word he did outpour.
Nothing farther then he uttered—not a feather then
   he fluttered—

Till I scarcely more than muttered "Other friends have flown before—
On the morrow **he** will leave me as my hopes have flown before."

   Then the bird said "Nevermore!"

Startled at the stillness broken by reply so aptly spoken,
"Doubtless," said I, "what it utters is its only stock
    and store
Caught from some unhappy master whom unmerciful Disaster

Followed fast and followed faster till his songs one burden bore—
Till the dirges of his Hope that melancholy burden bore
    Of 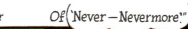'Never—Nevermore.'"

But the Raven still beguiling my sad fancy into
    smiling,
Straight I wheeled a cushioned seat in front of bird,
    and bust and door;

Then, upon the velvet sinking, I betook myself to
    linking
Fancy unto fancy, thinking what this ominous bird
    of yore —

What this grim, ungainly, ghastly, gaunt, and ominous
    bird of yore
    Meant in croaking "Nevermore."

This I sat engaged in guessing but no syllable expressing
To the fowl whose fiery eyes now burned into my bosom's
    core;
This and more I sat divining, with my head at ease reclining

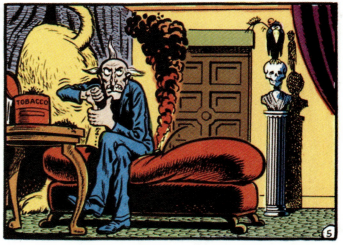

On the cushion's velvet lining that the lamp-light gloated o'er,
But whose velvet-violet lining with the lamp-light gloating o'er,

She shall press, ah, nevermore!

Then, methought, the air grew denser, perfumed from an unseen censer
Swung by seraphim whose foot-falls tinkled on the **tufted floor**.
"Wretch," I cried, "thy God hath lent thee — by these angels he hath sent thee

Respite — respite and nepenthe from the memories of Lenore;
Quaff, oh quaff this kind nepenthe and forget this lost Lenore!"

Quoth the Raven ("Nevermore.")

"Prophet!" said I, "thing of evil! — prophet still, if bird or devil! —
Whether Tempter sent, or tempest tossed thee here ashore,
Desolate yet all undaunted, on this desert land enchanted —

On this home by Horror haunted — tell me truly, I implore —
Is there — **is** there balm in Gilead? — tell me — tell me, I implore!"

Quoth the Raven ("Nevermore.")

"Prophet!" said I, "thing of evil! — prophet still, if bird or devil!
By that heaven that bends above us — by that God we both adore —

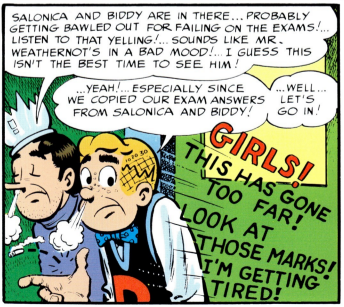

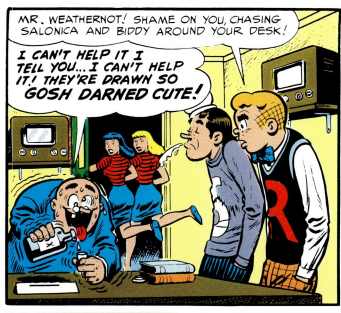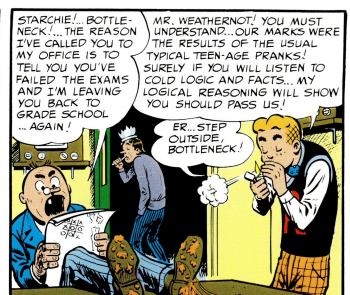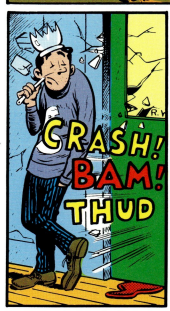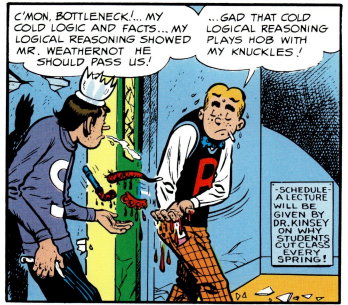

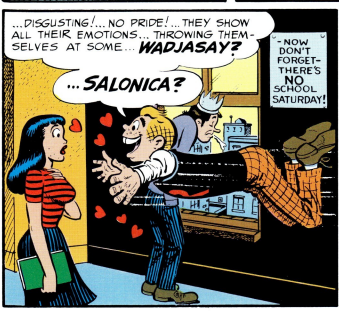
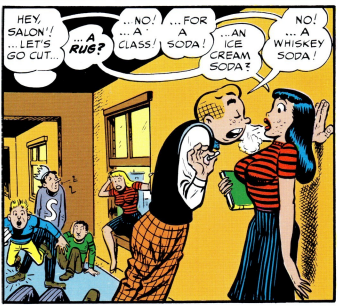

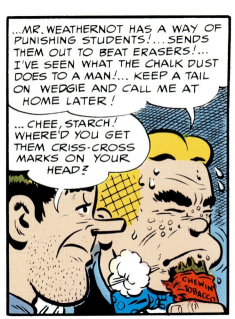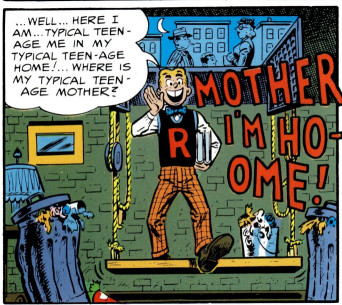

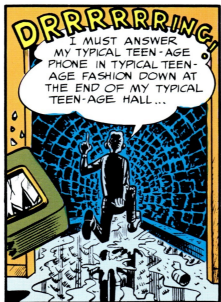

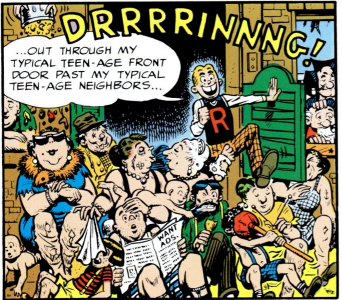
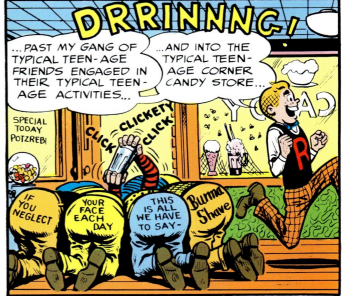

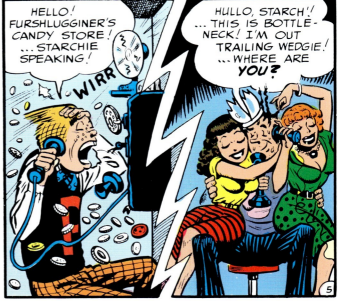

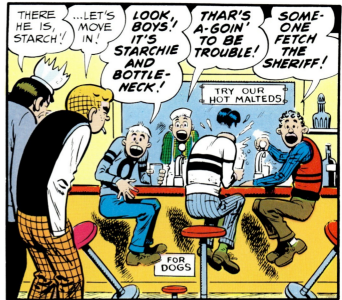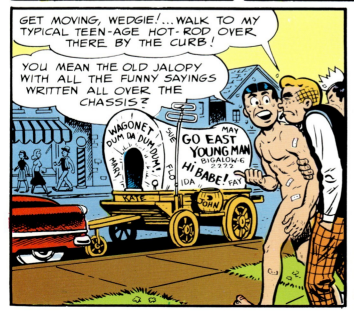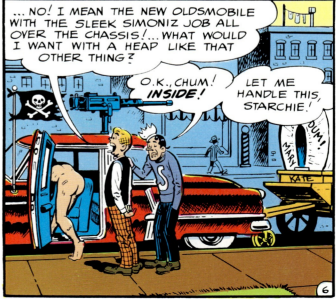

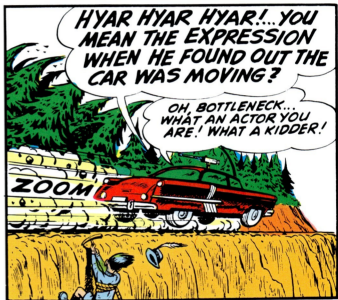

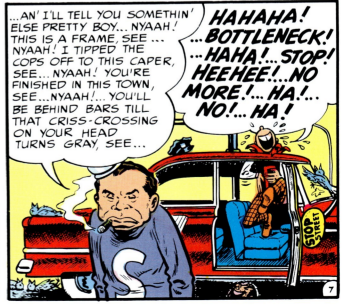

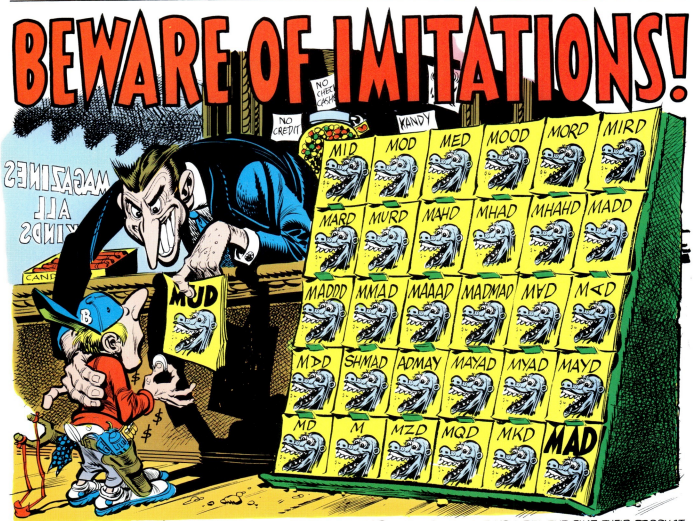

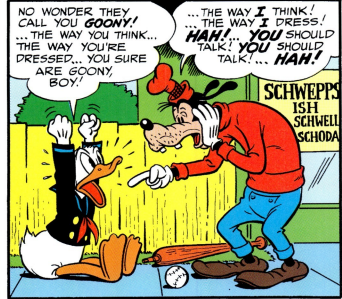

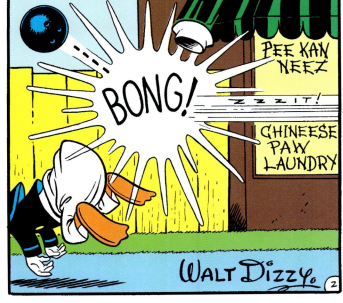

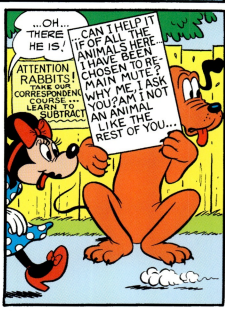
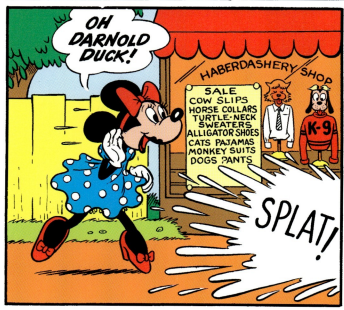

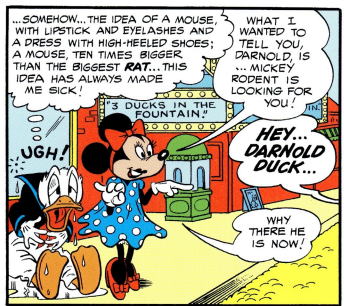

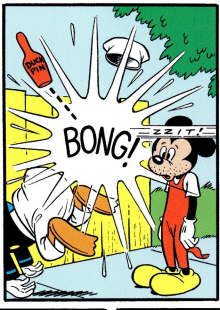

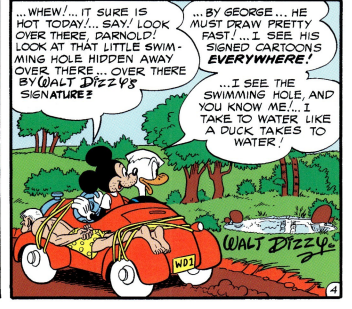

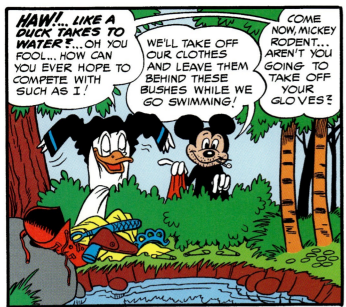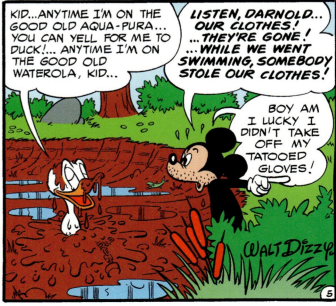

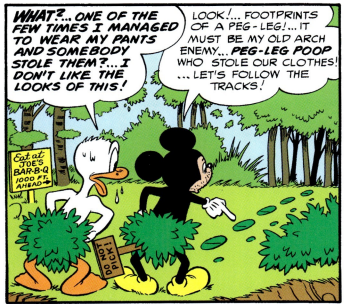

T.V. DEPT.: OUR CONSTANT READERS HAVE NO DOUBT NOTICED OUR SUDDEN SHIFT TO TELEVISION! WE *ARE* GIVING SPECIAL ATTENTION TO T.V. BECAUSE WE BELIEVE IT HAS BECOME AN INTEGRAL PART OF LIVING... A POWERFUL INFLUENCE IN SHAPING THE FUTURE... BUT MAINLY WE ARE GIVING ATTENTION BECAUSE WE JUST GOT A NEW T.V. SET!... SO HERE'S OUR STORY...

HOWDY-DOOIT!

NO! LET ME GO! THAT'S *MY* SUNRAY FROM *MY* MOVIES BEHIND HIS HEAD AND I *WANNIT* BACK!

BILL Elder.

LIBERACE • DIAL 'M' FOR MURROW • THE BUTTONS SHOW • BREAK THE BANK • KIDDIE PROGRAMS

HEY KIDS...

POW
SOK

...WHAT TIME IS IT?

HEY SHLOIMY!

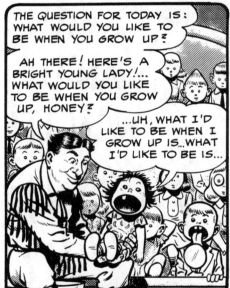

BEWARE OF IMITATIONS!

BEWARE OF IMITATIONS!... COMPARE THE TWO MAGAZINES ABOVE!... WHICH ONE IS THE DIRTY IMITATION? MANY OF OUR COMPETITORS ARE PUTTING OUT MAGAZINES THAT ARE IMITATIONS... FILTHY UNAMERICAN SWIPES OF *MAD* MAGAZINE... IF YOU WANT TO AVOID IMITATIONS... MAKE THIS SIMPLE TEST...

First... roll up a *MAD* magazine! Light it! Take a couple puffs!... Notice how slowly the paper burns!... Notice how gently it sets your head on fire!

...Now, take any other magazine and light it!... Notice the oily brown poisonous coloring of the smoke... the hotness of the melted staples on your tongue!

...Yes... once you make this test, we guarantee you will never smoke an imitation magazine again... You will never do *nuttin'* ever again!

REMEMBER!... MAD IS MILDER... MUCH MILDER!

1955-1959

July, 1955: "Rock Around the Clock," by Bill Haley and the Comets, slots in as *Billboard* magazine's number one record, and stays there for eight weeks—an event that will come to be regarded as the start of the rock 'n' roll era. The number one hit of the year, however, will prove to be "Cherry Pink and Apple Blossom White," by Perez Prado and his orchestra. A brand-new amusement park, Disneyland, is built for a staggering $17 million, causing some naysayers to refer to it as "Walt's Folly." Two-thirds of the homes in America now have television sets. And *MAD* makes its debut as a magazine.

The "extremely important message" referred to on the cover of *MAD*'s first magazine issue can be found on the first page of the book you are now holding. It takes but a glance at the fretful editors depicted there to realize that, in fact, they weren't kidding!

The Jack Davis cover to issue #27 (April, 1956) is a veritable cornucopia of fifties-era personalities. As if in deliberate contrast to that claustrophobically "busy" cover, Wallace Wood's "Spring Issue" cover (#28, July, 1956) is the very model of simplicity.

Wood's "circus poster" cover of #29 (the first Al Feldstein-edited issue, September, 1956) was printed with just two colors (red and black) as a means of cutting back on production expenses. No such austerity program was in force for the next issue's cover, which featured Norman Mingo's archetypal rendering of Alfred E. Neuman (#30, December, 1956). This painting is the single most-recycled image of Alfred, having appeared countless times over the past forty years on various *MAD*-related licsensed products.

Of the next seven Mingo-illustrated covers, especially noteworthy are the Mount Rushmore cover of issue #31 (with the bermuda-shorts-wearing nuclear family standing alongside their '57 Ford Fairlane), the "Egyptian tomb" cover of issue #32, and Mingo's *MAD* magnum opus, the "Special 5th Anniversary" cover of issue #35. Packed into this double-spread cover are virtually all of the best-known advertising icons and celebrity spokespersons of the era, including Uncle Ben, the Jolly Green Giant, the Smith Bros., Aunt Jemima, Betty Crocker, the Campbell Soup Kids, Mr. Peanut, Speedy Alka-Seltzer, Elsie the Cow, and dozens more.

The first cover artist to work for *MAD* during Mingo's extended hiatus was not a human, but rather a simian named J. Fred Muggs, who was well-known at the time as Dave Garroway's sidekick on the original *Today* show. While J. Fred Muggs was undeniably cute, he had a reputation for being cantankerous—a reputation he lived up to while finger-painting the cover of #38 (March, 1958). Perhaps in protest of an editorial suggestion not to his liking, J. Fred took a bite out of Al Feldstein. Muggs did no further work for *MAD*.

Noted illustrator C. C. Beall contributed the cover of *MAD*'s 39th issue (May, 1958), a montage of celebrities that collectively form the visage of Alfred E. Neuman.

Science fiction illustrator Kelly Freas took over as *MAD*'s cover artist with issue #40 (July, 1958). Assistant editor Jerry De Fuccio had bumped into Freas, and referred him back to Feldstein; Freas would do every cover through the end of the decade. While Mingo could flawlessly execute endless cookie-cutter versions of Alfred's face, Freas preferred to keep his Alfreds playfully impish, changing the facial expressions as each piece dictated. This often did not sit well with Feldstein, who wanted an instantly recognizable mascot with which to anchor the magazine. While Kelly's fifties-era covers are all uniformly well crafted, his *pièce de résistance* is unquestionably the artfully done "scarecrow" painting that adorns the cover of issue #43 (December, 1958).

Two Elder-illustrated ad parodies appear in this color section. The first, "Canadian Clubbed," (#26, November, 1955) is a takeoff on a then-popular series of print ads for Canadian Club whiskey. A companion piece, "Beer Belongs— Enjoy It!," appeared on the back cover of the following issue (#27, April, 1956).

"*MAD* Record Labels" (#32, April, 1957) dates from a time of transition in pop music; while rock 'n' rollers like Elvis Presley, Buddy Holly, and the Everly Brothers had a lock on the Hit Parade's top slots, older and more traditional artists still commanded huge followings. *MAD*'s juxtaposition of the new and old styles make for some inspired pairings: Fats Domino with the NBC Orchestra, Arturo Toscanini conducting Bill Haley's Comets, and "Slaughter on 10th Avenue" by Kate Smith.

Joe Orlando's "Reader's Disgust" spoof (#33, June, 1957) is one of only two color paintings Orlando ever did for *MAD*. The "Winsten" cigarette ad (#37, January, 1958) represents two *MAD* "firsts": the first use of photography in an ad parody, and the first use of staffers playing parts. (The postman is Nick Meglin, while the irate man in the sweater is Jerry De Fuccio.) The Kelly Freas-illustrated "Sailem" ad (#40, July, 1958) marks the first *MAD* piece to have an anti-smoking slant. The message was delivered more firmly in the "Awaysis" cigarette ad that appears later in this section (from #48, July, 1959).

Two of Freas's best-remembered parodies finish out this color section. The "Crust" ad (#43, December, 1958) skewers Crest toothpaste's "Look, Ma, no cavities!" campaign. "Great Moments in Medicine" (#48, July, 1959) is widely regarded as his single best *MAD* parody. Noteworthy are the horrified faces on the patient and his family, the attending physician's barely concealed glee, and the array of Draconian-looking medical instruments on the nightstand.

"Anyone Can Build This Coffee Table" (from #24) introduces the magazine version of Kurtzman's humor. Note the sustained repetition of certain key words or phrases, a Kurtzman trademark. Note how Davis's pictures perfectly compliment the text. Note how Harvey has influenced the writing of this paragraph!

The "Ed Suvillan Show" article (#27, illustrated by Elder) pokes fun at the legendary CBS variety show, which ran on Sunday nights from 1948 to 1971. Sullivan's "really big shew" presented important early TV appearances by such performers as Bob Hope, Dinah Shore, Martin and Lewis, Elvis Presley (shot from the waist up to avoid his gyrating pelvis), and Eddie Fisher.

"Scenes We'd Like to See," written and illustrated by

Phil Interlandi, was a popular feature in the early *MAD* magazines; "The Fighter Who Didn't Rally" (from #27) appears here. When Interlandi departed with Kurtzman to work on the short-lived *Trump*, Joe Orlando and George Woodbridge continued the feature. Orlando is represented here by "The Faithful Dog" (#32), while Woodbridge's entry is "Driving the Golden Spike" (#51, December, 1959).

Two early pieces written and illustrated by Al Jaffee (who would later become one of *MAD*'s most valuable assets) are included in this section: "My Secret" (#26) and "Stamps" (#28).

Stan Freberg contributed two articles to the early *MAD*. The first, "Anyone for Wrist Slashing?" (illustrated by Wood, #25, September, 1955), appears here. Ernie Kovacs was another early celebrity contributor. An avid fan, Kovacs was said to carry copies of *MAD* around with him to ruffle the feathers of fellow patrons at such posh New York night spots as the Stork Club and "21." After Kurtzman and company's departure, Feldstein kept the "celebrity guest" tradition going. Kovacs contributed a series of takeoffs on "Ripley's Believe it or Not!" entitled "Strangely Believe It!"; two examples appear here. Kelly Freas's likeness of the cigar-loving Kovacs appears in the "Barker 61" ad parody from earlier in this section (#38). (This parody did not involve any actual input from Kovacs, however.) Other celebrity pieces include Tom Lehrer's "The Wild West Is Where I Want to Be" (#32), Danny Kaye's "The New Baby" (#43), Bob and Ray's "Pressure Can Report" (#47, June, 1959), and Sid Caesar's "The Professor Lectures on Space" (#47). In a hold-over of comic-book custom, *MAD* didn't start listing writer's by-lines (apart from celebrities) until the end of the fifties, when it became obvious that the magazine should be giving credit where credit was due.

"Free-Fall Ferris," written by Jerry De Fuccio and illustrated by Wood (issue #29), is among the first pieces written for *MAD* after Kurtzman's exit. From this point onward, all the material in this book is post-Kurtzman.

"Alfred E. Neuman Answers Your Questions" (from #29) marks the first appearance of Don Martin, who quickly came to be regarded as "*MAD*'s maddest artist." Other Martin pieces in this section include "Future TV Ad" (#32), "Feeding Pigeons Homemade Popcorn" (#33, June, 1957), and "The Seaside Incident" (#35). Taken collectively, these early pieces reveal a macabre and darkly sexual side of Martin's work that was never seen again in his later sound-effect-oriented work.

"Elvis Pelvis" takes off on fifties show biz phenomenon Elvis Presley (from #30). Jack Davis manages to perfectly capture Elvis's trademark sneer. Also from #30 (and illustrated by Davis) is "Bowling," which was Nick Meglin's very first *MAD* article. Another Meglin article, "Baseball Is Ruining Our Children" (#34, August, 1957), is an early *MAD* classic. (This piece, and the reason behind it, is discussed at length in the foreword to *MAD About the Sixties*.)

"Why I Left the Army and Became a Civilian" is Frank Jacobs's very first *MAD* article (from issue #33). Jacobs quickly became one of *MAD*'s most prolific contributors, and would later be known by the cognoscenti as *MAD*'s "poet laureate." Two other Jacobs pieces appear in this section. "*MAD* Goes Hi-Fi" (#37, illustrated by Bob Clarke) touches upon the audiophile craze initiated by the improved "high fidelity" sound quality and longer playing times made possible by the introduction of 33 1/3 r.p.m. records. "Comic Book Heroes Taken from Real Life" (#48, illustrated by Wood) pokes fun at Conrad Hilton, Wernher von Braun, Prince Charles, Dick Nixon, and Jimmy Hoffa. The "Bonnie Prince Charlie" strip caused a scandal when it was reprinted by a British tabloid; *MAD*'s desecration of the Royal Family was not at all appreciated by the British subjects.

"The *MAD* Primer" (by writer Tom Koch and artist Joe Orlando) is *MAD*'s update of the "Dick and Jane" textbook series created in 1927 (#41, September, 1958). This was the first of many such "primers" on various subjects; also appearing here is "The *MAD* Horror Primer," which ties in to the late fifties monster movie craze (#49, September, 1959, written by Larry Siegel and masterfully illustrated by Wood).

"*MAD* Playgrounds" is a fine example of writer/artist Dave Berg's early *MAD* work (#50, October, 1959). The debut of the "Lighter Side" feature, for which Berg became best known, is still several years away.

The "Hames" underwear ad (*MAD* #51) references the scandalous 1958 love triangle involving singer Eddie Fisher, his movie-star wife Debbie Reynolds, and then-reigning sex goddess Elizabeth Taylor. Considered "America's sweethearts," Fisher and Reynolds went to console their friend Taylor after her husband, Mike Todd, was killed in a plane crash; Fisher never left. The public outcry against Fisher and Taylor's pairing was so negative that Fisher's career would never quite recover.

Another fifties sex kitten appears in the "American Expense Account Cheques" ad parody (from #43), French actress Brigitte Bardot. In films such as *...And God Created Woman*, the angelic-looking Bardot would inevitably exchange her clothes for a loosely wrapped towel, as pictured in the parody.

"Teenage Magazine," by Siegel and Orlando (#51), points up how quickly the youth-oriented rock 'n' roll subculture had become a societal force. In an era of "Oo, Ee, Oo, Ah Ah"-style rock lyrics, Siegel's suggestion to use eye charts for songwriting inspiration seems a particularly apt one.

We conclude with the "Cell Telephone System" ad (#49), a juxtaposition of Bell Telephone's advertising push to encourage long distance usage and the "phone booth stuffing" fad that swept college campuses in 1959. The Kelly Freas art is a direct takeoff on a widely circulated *Life* magazine photograph (taken on a college campus in California) of a fully stuffed phone booth.

By the close of the fifties, *MAD* magazine had become a firmly established entity in the publishing world, and in the American scene at large. While there was no particular concern about *MAD*'s future, there was also no particular reason to think that *MAD*'s success would go on forever. Publishing could sometimes be a tricky business—as Bill Gaines found out the hard way with the premature burial of his EC comic book line. All the *MAD*-men could do to help ensure their own survival was to keep their noses firmly to the proverbial (and, in this case, satirical) grindstone, and to emerge at the end of each month or so having ground out another 48 pages of choice *MAD*-ness.

Fortunately for them (and happily for us), that is exactly what they did—and have continued to do for an astounding forty-five years.

What—them worry?

—Grant Geissman

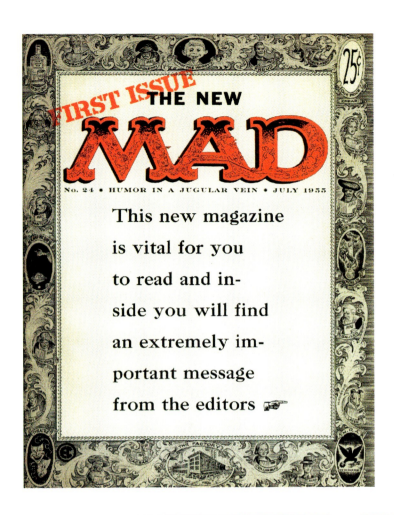
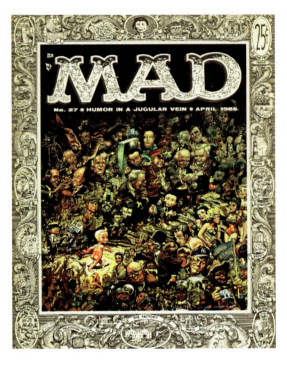
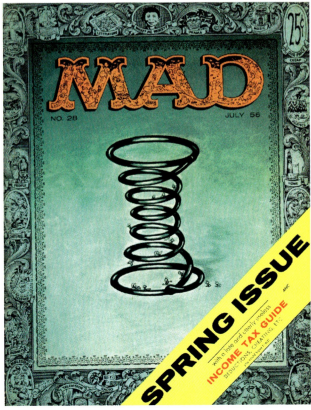
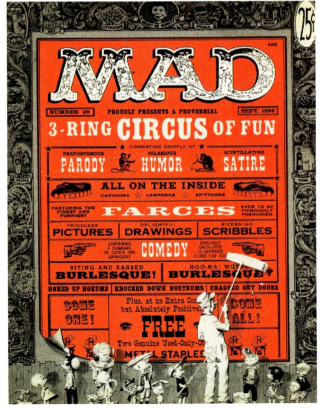

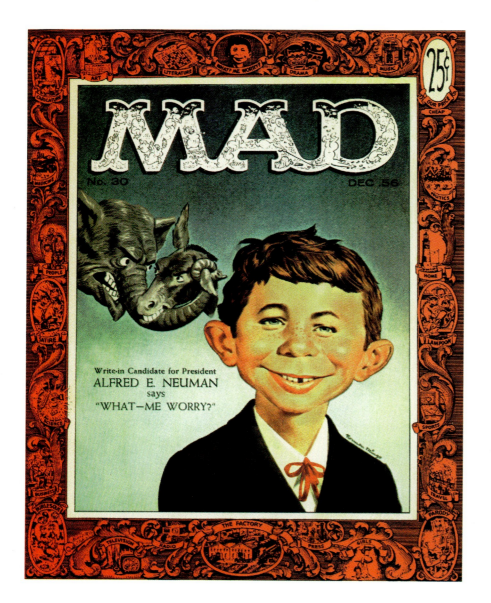

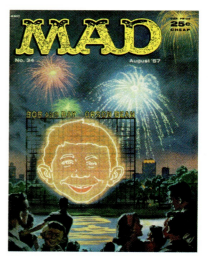
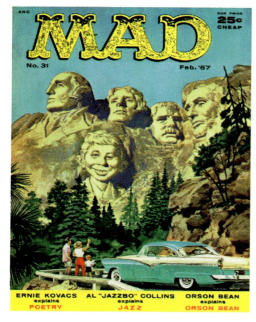
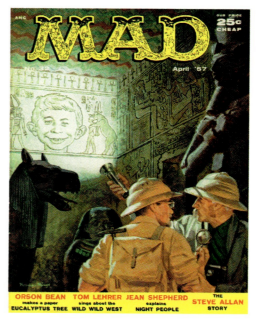

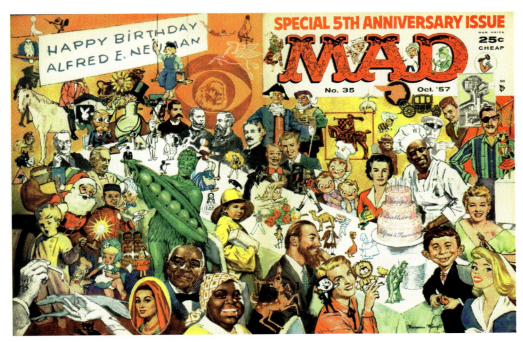
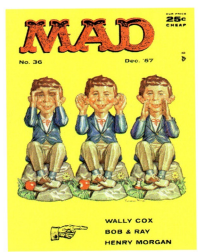

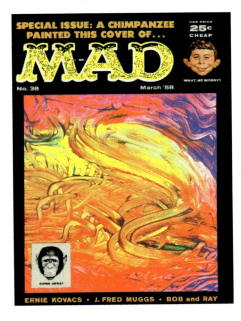
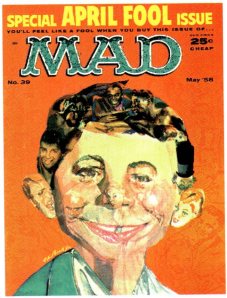

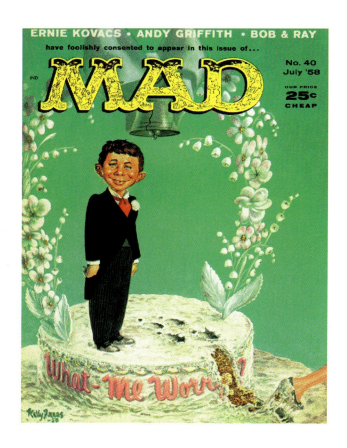
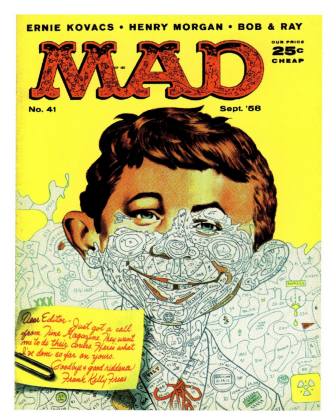
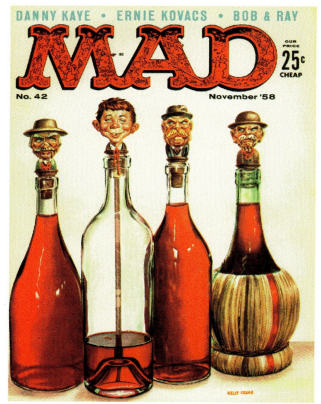
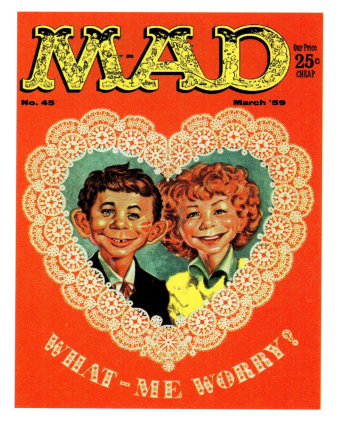

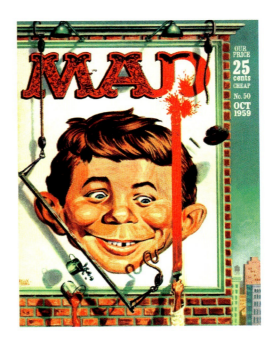
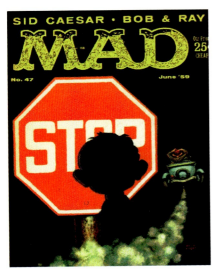
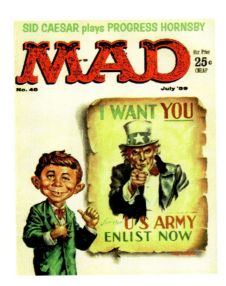

it's HIGH ADVENTURE

When you bird watch for the Pipit!

1 "**It is not without danger** to birdwatch for the Meadow Pipit!" writes an American friend of Canadian Clubbed. "Many's the time one blunders and stumbles through the dense underbrush in pursuit of what he thinks to be the Meadow Pipit only to discover he has been following the Tree Pipit. We had been crashing through the dense underbrush of the Bronx Botanical Gardens all day on the trail of the wily Meadow Pipit. My host, Sir Covert Scapular who was in the lead of our party from the Concourse Manor was suddenly observed to stiffen, his eyes riveted directly ahead of him. With joyous cries, we all rushed forward to share his discovery ... a Planter's Peanut wrapper you can send away for premiums."

2 "**I acted quickly** shouting 'halfies!' before the others could gather wits. We resumed our birdwatch. It was here Sir Covert Scapular showed his birdwatch prowess indicating what seemed to be a daub of mud, or an insect construction, which was in reality *the nest of the Meadow Pipit!*"

3 "**Joyously tootling** our bird whistles we rushed forward. For there is nothing like delicious Pipit eggs. You can whip a Pipit egg or even dip it, or dip a whipped Pipit egg for the dipped whippit is pipped, or rather dipped whipped pip dippit, but I digress. So there we were, crashing towards the nest of the Meadow Pipit which looked like a daub of mud or an insect construction. Imagine our surprise when we found that it really was an insect construction."

4 "**In no time flat** we were back at the Manor sipping Canadian Clubbed to mainly kill pain of stings. After the 12th drink imagine my surprise to find my host, Sir Covert Scapular was in reality ... a Meadow Pipit!"

5 **Which all goes to show** that whatever part of the world you visit, whether it be Timbuktu or the Bronx Botanical Gardens ... you will always find that drink that has been a popular favorite amongst connoisseurs for generations, you will find that ever popular drink, Coca Cola. Canadian Clubbed too, is famous all over because it is *light* as scotch, *rich* as rye, *satisfying* as bourbon with distinctive character and flavor and like that. And mainly you get tight.

IN 87 LANDS ... THE BEST IN THE IGLOO

"Canadian Clubbed" 6 YEARS OLD PLENTY PROOF

IMPORTED WHISKEY MADE BY JEETER LESTER

IMPORTED FROM CANADA. OUR MOTTO: DRINK ENOUGH CANADIAN CLUBBED AND YOU'LL DRINK CANADA DRY.

"Visiting The Grandparents" by William Elder. Number 1 in the series "Ol' Home Life"

While you are visiting—
What makes a glass of beer taste so good?

Malted barley—with important body minerals plus liquid matter. For thing that makes glass of beer taste so good is terrible thirst.

Tangy hops. Yes—visiting can be a series of tangy hops if you play your cards right. And you'd be surprised how good free beer tastes!

The way it "goes with everything"—makes beer this country's Beverage of Moderation—the way it fits into our friendly way of life—the way each glass makes us friendlier and friendlier and friendlier.

Beer Belongs—Enjoy It!

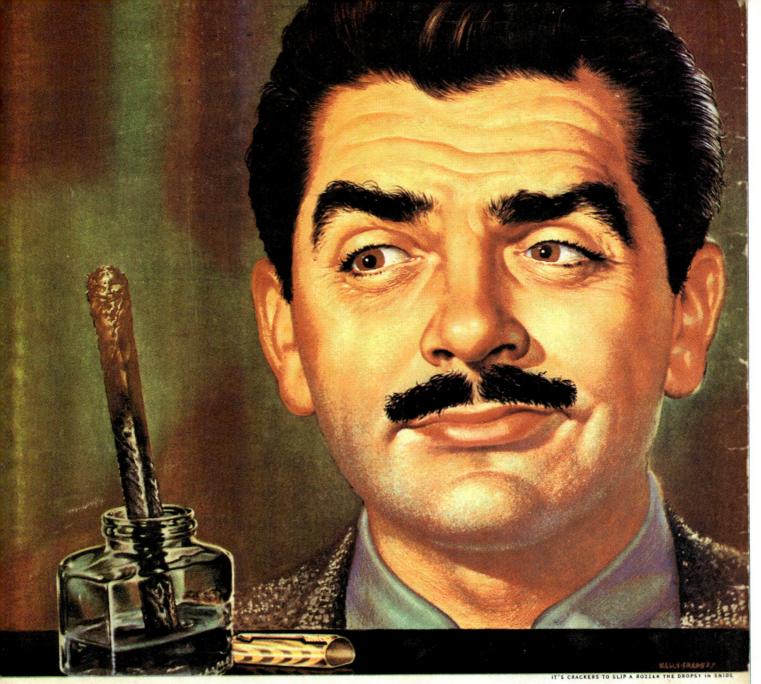

IT'S CRACKERS TO SLIP A ROZZER THE DROPSY IN SNIDE

New kind of cigar even fills itself by itself—with ink

The man is watching something revolutionary happen—his unique new Barker 61 literally drinking up ink all by itself by capillary "suction." He has simply removed the band-clip and set the cigar in the ink bottle upside down. In just 10 seconds the cigar is full. Now he'll lift the Barker 61 from the ink. No wiping needed because ink can't cling to this special tobacco surface. The perfect item for signing contracts in smoke-filled conference rooms. This totally new use of a cigar is just one of the many wonders of the Barker 61. F'rinstance, you can even fill your cigars with Dry Martinis. Then you'll be able to smoke and drink in one sinful labor-saving operation. Whatever you use it for, you'll like the classy beauty of the Barker 61 Cigar. (Talk about classy, isn't this a classy ad, not even mentioning who the guy is?)

Actually, man in picture is not who you think it is, but a double bearing a startling likeness who we got much cheaper.

Barker 61
Capillary Cigar

Unlike any cigar in this world

A new idea in smoking!

Sailem ...don't inhalem

- **menthol fuel**
- **a hull of a pack**
- **filtered smokestack, too**

Sparkling water . . . radiant air . . . Spring! The perfect scene to try a new idea in smoking. Instead of inhaling, try sailing Sailem Cigarettes. Then, the worst you can develop is a cold. Actually, we're not even in the tobacco business. We wanna hook you on the sailing habit. Try Sailems. You'll want a yacht!

Created by Chris-Craft Boat Co.
Runabout Cigarette Pack Div.

"Look, Mom—no more cavities!"

Crust Gumpaste helps gums take the place of teeth by coating them with a hard white enamel finish! Just the thing for punks who get their teeth knocked out from running around with teen-age gangs.

Fluidsteel is a trademark for Proctor & Rumble's exclusive liquid metal gum-coater.

© 1958, The Proctor & Rumble Co.

PRESENTING THE BILL—*reproduced here, is one of a series of original oil paintings, "Practising Medicine For Fun and Profit", commissioned by Park-David.*

Great Moments in Medicine

Once the crisis has passed . . . once the patient has regained his strength . . . once the family is relieved and grateful . . . that's the time when the physician experiences one of the great moments in medicine. In fact, the *greatest moment* in medicine! Mainly, the moment when he presents his bill! That's the time when all of the years of training and study and work seem worthwhile. And there's always the chance that the shock might mean more business for him!

Park-David scientists are proud of their place in the history of practicing medicine for fun and profit, helping to provide doctors with the materials that mean higher fees and bigger incomes. For example, our latest development . . . tranquilizer-impregnated bill paper . . . designed to eliminate the shock and hysteria that comes when the patient gets a look at your bill. Not only will he remain calm when he sees what you've charged . . . now he won't even *care!*

COPYRIGHT 1959—PARK-DAVID & COMPANY, WITH THE BLESSINGS OF THE AMA

PARK-DAVID ... *Pioneers in bigger medical bills*

DO IT YOURSELF DEPT.

Anyone can build this Coffee Table

With comparatively little trouble, the useful and attractive coffee-table pictured here, complete, can be yours or anybody elses if you're willing to take the time to build it yourself...if you're willing to get a few calloused on your hands...if you're willing to get a little sawdust in your hair...if you're willing to lose a couple of fingers.

There's no trick to building a coffee table, complete, like this. All you need is a few fundamental tools, some odds and ends from the hardware store, a good right arm, the will to work, and mainly, coffee. Check on the coffee first since if nobody in your house drinks coffee, there's no sense building this coffee table.

Now...the initial step in building this coffee table, then, is to arrange for time to build this thing. If you can't find time during the evenings or the weekends...quit work. A week or two will do it. Remember...you'll be *saving* money by building this table. If you can't leave your job you might hire a contractor to come in and build the coffee table. Don't be afraid to *go out and get this thing done.*

However you decide, on the following pages are twelve basic steps to follow to build this coffee table, complete. So roll up your sleeves, get out your nails, your hammers, and your band aides...and go watch television.

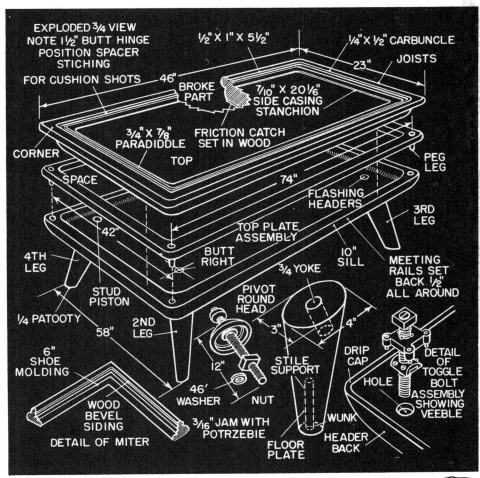

CONTINUED

COFFEE TABLE CONTINUED

1. Lumber. Select your lumber with a careful eye for imperfections such as checks, bows and knots. If you can't get well seasoned, finishing grade basswood, mahogany or teak at your lumber yard, you will find that cheese-boxes and orange-crate ends will do very nicely as a substitute.

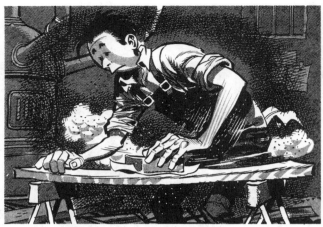

2. Sandpapering. The success or failure of a piece very often depends on the sanding. In order to work gradually up to the smoothest finish, start with grit size No. 1/0 and work up to grit size No. 2/0. Then go to next finer grit size No. 3/0 and thence to an even finer grit size of 4/0.

3. More Sandpapering. You can't do enough sanding. You are up to very fine grit of 5/0 ... go to finer grit of 6/0 ... then to grit 6/0.5 and on to grit 6/0.05 and on to 6/0.005. Then comes very teenchy-weenchy grit, 6/0.6x, and after sanding with that, use teenchyest grit, $6/0\sqrt{00_2}$

4. Nailing. Now, back to our tools... (remember, all you need to build this coffee table, complete, are simple basic tools usually found in the average home) We assemble the main-brace cantilever carefully with our finishing nails and hammer. (a rock can be substituted for hammer)

5. Fastening. When the main-brace cantilever is assembled, we then bore ½" countersunk dowel pockets in each corner with our automatic drill. (surprisingly, an automatic drill is *really* a simple basic tool that *should* be in every average home) When dowel pocket is mortised properly... tenon.

6. Trim. Now take up the lumber for the table top and set it on your circular-saw power-tool top. (a *must* for every average home... I mean, let's face it! If you want to do things right, you can't be a cheap skate) Set miter gauge and select dado head to make self-aligning ogival rabbet.

7. Final Assembly. Your most important step is to then stamp the table-top support out of 1/8" steel sheet on your sheet-metal press. This done, fit toggle-bolts to butt-hinges bevelled to corrugated fasteners. Clinch core with trunnions and hoist the mizzenmast to the starboard tack.

8. Sandpapering. When the toggle-bolts are fitted, the job is completed. Back to sanding. Start with the last fine grit size you used and work back down, to coarsest grit size, No. 1/0. You can never do enough sanding. Success or failure depends on sanding. Don't forget, plenty of sanding!

9. More Sandpapering. Keep sanding! Get right back there and keep on sanding! There's never enough sanding! Stay in there and keep sanding. Don't stop sanding!

10. Keep Sanding!

11. Finishing. And now, to give final touches to finish the coffee table, complete, pictured on page 35, we varnish, steel wool, and pumice all surfaces... bury a caladium bulb in soil, which we can make by decaying leaves for no less than a year and fashion a clay pot while bulb takes root.

12. Pièce de Résistance. We pot the full grown caladium plant and place it on the table and there we have our coffee table, complete, pictured on page 35 with exception of pack of cigarettes you see on the table. We will show you how to make the pack of cigarettes in the next issue.

END

CONFIDENTIAL INFORMATION DEPT.

Next...a treat!...the kind of magazine reading that's sweeping the country, where we expose confidential information and dig up all kinds low-down you can run tattle about! There'll be lusty gossiping o'er the back fences tonight when you read the following skeletons we rooted from the closets...Forinstance...

WAS GEORGE

"I cannot tell a lie, Pa...I cut down the cherry tree with my little hatchet..." Did he really say it? Was it a cherry tree? Did he really use a little hatchet? Who was covering up?

This is the picture that the ones who are covering up have wanted you to believe. But if you want to know the real unvarnished truth, take a good look-erola at the picture to the right of this one...

This is our own exclusive picture with eyeglasses right back where they belong, wig removed along with false wooden teeth. Now decide for yourself if someone hasn't handed you the phonus-bolonus!

An irrefutable document. The signature: James MacKay, British commander. Below it the signature of fellow British officer before he conveniently decided to switch allegiance; G. W. Washington.

WASHINGTON "GEORGE"?

Was he 'george'?.. to use a popular expression meaning was he O.K.? What's the straight dope about the man who was allowed to lead our boys against the King of England? Well, cackle over this one:

In 1759, who do you think appealed for—quote—"the heroic spirit of every free-born Englishman to attest the rights and privileges of our King." A quote from Cornwallis or Burgoyne? Hold on to your hats because it was our own G.G.W. who dropped those pearls of advice. And who do you think he was getting his combat pay from at the time Braddock was his top-kick? King Georgie, of course.

Those are the facts. Add them up yourself. If one and one makes two it's clear some one is covering up the real facts about how the revolutionary war was won. But here's something even more sensational for you to snivel about.

G.G.W. was no slouch with the women. While he was putting the engagement ring on Martha with one hand, with the other he was writing love letters like this: "... I profess myself a votary of love... you have drawn me, dear Madam...into an honest confession of a simple Fact... doubt it not, nor expose it..." What's wrong with a little old love letter you say? Hold on to your tricorns. This little missive was written to George's *neighbor's wife!*

Which all goes to prove how we, with our fearless investigatory methods, can dig up the hushed-up facts on this man's life... which all goes to prove how we can dig up hushed-up facts on *any* man's life.

And by golly, don't think we haven't got the hushed-up facts on *all* YOU out there.

So watch out!

They want you to believe he stood in the boat like this...

We believe standing would have rocked it over like this.

WHO IS COVERING UP? CONTINUED

CONFIDENTIAL INFO. CONTINUED

Continuing our confidential information article...we next include the type feature that is always good for a leer or two...you know the type, it goes something like this...

HAVE YOU HEARD ABOUT John Smith And His Indian Princess

The boys sent him out to barter trinkets and beads for fish, fowl and corn... But (haw!) it seems that the copper-hued Algonquin maidens (snicker!) were more his (guffaw!) dish.

What was Powhatan covering up?

COURTESY OF N.Y. PUBLIC LIBRARY

Famous picture of Pocahontas saving John Smith. Why didn't the big boys who are covering up . . . rather than show you a phoney picture of Pocahontas looking like this . . .

Why didn't they show you 12 year old Pocahontas looking like this . . . our exclusive, truthful picture of Pocahontas.

For the past 350 years, the hottest scandal of the century has been kept hush-hush until now. For 350 years, John Q. Public has been told that John Smith was rescued by a romantically inclined Indian princess named Pocahontas whose poppa, Powhatan, had ordered Smith's brains bashed out. But the full story that John Q. Public doesn't know is one that had the settlers buzzing from the Werowocomo to the Pawmunkey.

We don't know what they called it then, but what we call it now is "robbing the cradle." For the simple fact is Pocahontas at the time was a tender, 12 years of age.

The record speaks for itself in John's own handwriting when he wrote in 1618, ". . . the King's most deare and wel-beloued daughter, being but a childe of twelue or thirteene yeeres of age." Furthermore, from his friends records, ". . . shee was . . . not past 13 yeares of age. Verie ofte shee came . . . with what shee covld get for Captaine Smith; that euer loued and vsed all the Countrie well, but her especially he euer mvch respected." That's the way the record reads, and, even though it's hard to read because of the way words have "e"s on the ends and the 'v's are used for 'u's and vice-versa, the sitvatione is uerye obuiovse. And what does it all mean?

It all all adds up to the fact that somebody's been covering up! Why the very name, John Smith, is as phoney as a wooden nickel and is obviously an alias. It all adds up to the fact that John Q. Public has once more been taken!

CONFIDENTIAL INFO. CONTINUED

By George, ain't this fun? Our next article is real exclusive... While most articles are monotonously informative, this one's completely uninformative where we tell you everything about nothing.

Was Snow White

HERE'S THE STORY ON THE HOAX OF THE CENTURY ...THE SNOW WHITE *WHITE WASH*

Documentary proof. Here is a photograph of the original "Snow White" book. Only she wasn't so Snow White as the title so clearly indicates.

Are you one of the suckers that got sold a phoney bill of goods on Snow White? If you are, and you probably are, this article will put you straight. For years now, millions of people have been duped into believing that Snow White is the real name of a time-honored fairy-tale character who had a run-in with seven dwarfs. Acting on an anonymous tip, we've been investigating this story and have come up with some sensational facts, the most startling of which is that Snow White is an *alias*.

The true facts of the matter is that first of all, the name is not Snow White but is Snow *Drop* . . . Or if you really want to get technical, the name is Snee wittchen . . . obviously a name of foreign extraction.

Sneewittchen conveniently disappeared when Snow White and the Seven Dwarfs came along.

What we ask is . . . what happened to Snowdrop? Answer that, and you'll blow the lid off the scandal of the century. Obviously, somebody is covering up.

| DUMMCHEN? | FRÖHLICH? | DOKTOR? | BRUMMBÄR? | NIESSEN? | SCHÜCHTERN? | SCHLAFHAUBE? |

Really Snow White?

Fiction: that it was a poisoned apple and a poisoned apple alone that torpedoed Snow White (Snowdrop)

Fact: that it was in truth as well as a poison apple a poisoned comb and a treacherously tightened corset.

Snow White quite forgot her promise to beware of strangers when the little old woman stopped at her door.

"Here's a Magic Wishing Apple, my dear," the old

Der gefiel dem Kind so gut, daß es sich bethören ließ und die Thür öffnete. Als es den Kamm gekauft hatte, sprach die Alte: „Nun will ich Dich auch kämmen." Snee=

A second element in the Snow White mystery is the seven dwarfs. Who are these dwarfs with their obviously underworld titles of Dopey, Happy, Doc, Grumpy, Sneezy, Bashful, and Sleepy? Translated into the foreign tongue the original Snowdrop appeared in, these names would be Dummchen, Fröhlich, Doktor, Brummbär, Niessen, Schüchtern, and Schlafhaube. Now get this little bit of interesting info.

In our thorough investigation of all the original works of Sneewittchen, nowhere did we turn up a single Dummchen, Fröhlich, Doktor, Brummbär, Niessen, Schüchtern or Schlafhaube.

Apparently, these seven dwarfs are imposters. That somebody is covering up the facts is unquestionable. That is one of the many plots going on around you day in and day out as we have proven in the past six pages is also unquestionable.

All that remains is for you, the people to do something! Act! Form groups! Write your congressman! But mainly, go kill yourself!

END

"Why anyone would find delight in reading (movie magazines)...will remain one of the world's great unsolved mysteries to me. I couldn't care less."

Stan Freberg

MAGAZINE DEPT.

Anyone for Wrist Slashing?

by Stan Freberg

I don't know about anybody else, but everytime I leaf through a movie magazine, its all I can do to keep from flailing my head against our used-brick fireplace in an effort to brainwash myself.

Why anyone would find delight in reading what "Tab Hunter's Favorite Vegetable Is," or "How June Allyson Finally Found Herself," or what "Sonny Tufts Wears To Bed," will remain one of the world's great unsolved mysteries to me. I couldn't care less. Still I am drawn like a ship to a rock full of sirens by these tales of trivia.

My first impulse upon reading something called "What it would be like to be Mrs. Rory Calhoun" was one of sheer panic. I was torn between hurling myself into a tub full of luke warm Yami Yogurt, or shaving my head and becoming a Trappist Monk. I do not even wish to know what it would be like to be Rory Calhoun, let alone MRS. This may seem to be an unorthodox attitude, as I am (in a rather small way) in the public eye. But I swear, honor bright, that if anybody from Modern Screen ever shows up at my house with a questionnaire and a camera, I shall beat them to within an inch of their life. (There will be a slight pause here while Modern Screen says "Don't worry pal, we never intended to.")

Comes now a story in the June issue of Silver Screen on Liz Taylor and titled; "REALLY! MISS TAYLOR." Really Miss Taylor is right. The authors would impress upon you (and I quote;) *"Liz may be charmingly confused by economy and cooking, but she's an 'old fashioned mother' whose home is her delight."*

SU - - - RE she is. She's like any "old fashioned mother" on your block. Listen:

"Elizabeth loves to greet the day sleeping late, breakfasting in bed, and going around the house with the sterling speed of a snail."

Commenting on her sparse wardrobe, the authors exclaim:

"You'd expect her wardrobe to be bulging with Parisian creations. A peek inside reveals exactly two French labels, more slacks than Evening Gowns, and one or two dresses that she wore when she was 14 years old. 'Of course' she confided, 'They no longer fit but I just can't bear to part with them.'"

On her "Old Fashionedness":

"She much prefers... cutting her own hair. If she notices a long strand in her short bob, she picks up whatever's handy, usually the manicure scissors, and proceeds to snip, hit or miss fashion."

On her Economy:

"When Liz spotted a bracelet she adored...a few weeks later she was considering a mink stole, but decided against buying it. 'Michael,' (Wilding) she said to her husband that evening, 'I've figured out a way I won't upset the budget, yet can buy the bracelet,...I didn't buy the mink stole, so I can use the money I saved on it to buy the bracelet.'

'That,' he announced, 'is the most amazing piece of logic I've ever heard!' but a week later, she had that bracelet in her Jewel box. It was a gift—from Michael."

Her youngest son (2 year old "Mikie") must be mighty durn proud to have such an every-day plain-old fashioned mother.

"Thank goodness he's such a good little boy and hasn't needed a spanking. His most serious pranks are pulling out light plugs and dialing phone numbers. The amazing thing is he often gets a real number and carries on a conversation!"

Her life is not without it's bitter disappointments:

"According to Michael, one of the nicest gifts Liz ever received, was an extra large T.V. set for the bedroom. Unfortunately, when they moved into their new home, her big luxury of lying in bed watching T.V. became a thing of the past. The bedrooms in their hillside house are located on a lower level, and they can't get any reception."

A bitter blow in any girl's life, I agree. She is also faced each day with problems that would make a less stalwart person snap under the strain. Consider the "Marble coffee table crisis:"

"It had me baffled"... Liz observed. "It weighs 550 pounds, is a free-form design, and measures eight feet at it's longest point. I had no idea when I had it designed that it wouldn't fit through the front door. Fortunately, the movers were alert fellows, and barely managed to squeeze the chunk of marble through a side door where the room was being remodeled."

I imagine you will rest easier, as indeed I did, to learn that the problem had been whipped.

She is not without an average American girl hobby or two, as revealed by the authors who, by their own admission, find Miss Taylor a tonic. They do not state what kind however.

"We've talked with Elizabeth many times and always find her a tonic. Once when we were lunching together, we asked what her favorite hobbies were. She replied; 'Jewelry and Houses.'"

On the subject of the latter:

"Each has been larger and more luxurious than the last. Their current house is done in excellent taste, even though it boasts a swimming pool in the FRONT yard."

The Wildings are not without their flair for the "dramatic":

"Their new home is done in beige with a 'dramatic' living room. Two glass walls, large stone fireplace and a tree growing in the corner."

Dramatic is right. It doesn't state what kind of tree, but you can bet it's no different from a tree like any other "old fashioned" mother might have growing in her living room. The astonishing thing about this whole article is that in several ways it closely parallels a screen play which I completed last February. The main characters, and indeed the very motif of the house are so similar that people might suspect I copied them after Miss Taylor and her ménage.

MAGAZINE DEPT. CONTINUED

WE GOT A TABLE HERE FOR MRS. WILTING.

Perish the thought! It is sheer chance, and any resemblance between Mr. and Mrs. Wilding and MY characters is not only coincidental, but outrageous that you should suggest it!

SCENE: Home of "Liz" Trailer, beautiful movie queen. A delivery man stands at the front door of her beige mansion. He is dripping wet having fallen head-long into the front yard swimming pool, which he did not expect to be there. He pushes the doorbell and the air is rent by giant chimes playing the theme from "A Place In the Sun." With a burst of tympani, the door slowly opens, tripping a circuit which floods the beige living room with indirect beige neon lighting. From the shadows steps a maid in a beige uniform, her beige face peering quizically at the intruder.

MAID: Yes?

DLVRY MAN: (Whistles appreciatively) That's quite an effect ya got here!

MAID: Yeah, it's a dramatic living room, ain't it? I see yer wet.

DLVRY MAN: You're tellin' me I'm wet? Why don't they put the pool in the back-yard like everybody else?

MAID: Don't ask me, buster. That's a nasty flesh-wound on yer forehead. You hit the diving board?

DLVRY MAN: No the house. It sorta blends into the hills here. It's beige.

MAID: You're tellin' me it's beige? Whattaya want?

DLVRY MAN: We got a 550 pound, 8 foot free-form marble coffee table here for Miss Trailer. She home?

MAID: No, she's in bed, having breakfast. She likes to greet the day by sleeping late.

DLVRY MAN: How's that again?

MAID: Skip it. Where's the table?

DLVRY MAN: In the pool. See I was on the front end and I was backing toward the house.

MAID: Good lord! Don't just stand there! Get it out!

DLVRY MAN: Charlie and Ed have got a block and tackle on it. We'll have it out pretty quick. Where's it go?

Copyright 1955 by Stan Freberg

MAID: In the living room. Bring it right through here. (She turns toward the living room and blends into the motif.)

SCENE: Dissolves to Liz who is traveling up the stairs from the lower level, at the sterling speed of a snail. She is dressed in a purple strapless Don Loper Original. Her husband, Michael Wilting, stands at the head of the stairs, his arms outstretched.

LIZ: Michael!

MICHAEL: Liz! How lovely you look in that purple strapless Don Loper original.

LIZ: This old rag? I've had it since I was fourteen. Of course it no longer fits, but I just can't bear to part with it.

MICHAEL: What a thrifty little wife I have.

LIZ: (Putting a cigarette into her jeweled cigarette holder and lighting it with her solid gold lighter in the shape of the M.G.M. lion.) I'm just an old fashioned mother I guess, but I've figured out how to cut our budget this month. You know that Hope Diamond I want so much?

MICHAEL: Now Liz...

LIZ: (putting her fingers to his lips,) Hush. I've decided not to buy Miami Beach, and with the money I save on not buying Miami Beach I can get the diamond.

MICHAEL: (A look of sheer reverance breaking over his face,) Is there no end to your cleverness?

SOUND: CRASH!

LIZ: (screams!) (Michael runs to front door where the men have succeeded in ripping all the moulding off the seven foot front door, with the eight foot, 550 pound free-form marble coffee table.)

MICHAEL: What the devil's going on here?

DLVRY MAN: (Staggering under load) We got a table here for Mrs. Wilting.

LIZ: (Coming into scene like snail) Oooh! It's my

you read it in MAD

table, Michael. Isn't it beautiful? The marble glistens almost like it was wet!

MICHAEL: Well it won't fit through here! Bring the fool thing around the other side of the living room. (Men stagger back off porch while Liz and Michael walk into the dramatic beige living room Liz pulls the drapes, letting in the noonday sun and tripping the circuit which turns on the Hi-Fi system. Exhausted by the effort, she sinks onto a 12 foot beige ottoman, as a long playing applause record booms over the Hi-Fi. She bows graciously from the ottoman. In one corner of the room her young son "Mikie" swings by his feet from the lower branches of the tree which grows there. She calls to him;

LIZ: Get down Mikie. The blood is rushing to your head!

MAID: Let the child be, Mam. This room could use a little color.

LIZ: Where are you? I can't see you?

MAID: I'm over here, blending with the motif.

LIZ: Oh. (She picks up a pair of pinking shears and commences to chop at her hair, hit or miss fashion.)

MAID: You're going to ruin your hair, Mam. Why don't you let a barber do that?

LIZ: At a buck fifty a crack? No thank you. I'll do it myself.

MIKIE: (Climbing down from tree and embracing her) Oh mummy. You're just an old fashioned mother, and I'm thankful that you've raised me in an old fashioned way. I wouldn't trade you for all my General Motors stock!

SOUND: GRAAACK! (Room trembles, and a sound is heard, not unlike a ratchet.)

MIKIE: What is that sound, not unlike a ratchet?

LIZ: They're jacking up the bedrooms so I can lie in bed and watch T.V. It's my big luxury. Go pull some light plugs out and dial some phone numbers now.

MIKIE: WHEE! (He exits.)

MAID: (Picking apples from tree) You ought'nt to let him use the phone.

LIZ: Why not? He never reaches anyone.

MAID: Oh Yeah? He bought and sold Jamaica Park three times yesterday.

LIZ: Remind me to cut his allowance, Michael.

MICHAEL: (Sticking his head out of tree house in top of tree) Please dear, I'm studying a script!

(The deliverymen appear staggering and straining outside glass wall of living room. At that moment the hillside trembles again from the bedroom raising. Charlie and Ed flee in panic, (under the impression that the Russians have hit L.A.) leaving the lone delivery man to bear the entire weight of the coffee table. With a mighty crash he careens right through the glass wall of the living room, hurling glass like shrapnel and depositing the table under the tree with a thud.

LIZ: Not there, you idiot! It goes over here by the ottoman!

DLVRY MAN: (Groans.)

LIZ: Here here! You're bleeding all over the motif!

DLVRY MAN: I'm bleeding on my overalls too.

LIZ: Who cares about your overalls?

DLVRY MAN: I do. I've had them since I was 39 years old. Of course, they no longer fit, but I just can't bear to part with them.

LIZ: Oh well, the room could use a little color.

MAID: That's what I say.

SOUND: (Room trembles.)

MICHAEL: (Springing from tree-house and bounding out of room.) How can I concentrate? HOW CAN I CONCENTRATE??

DLVRY MAN: (Applying a tourniquet) What's that thing supposed to be?

LIZ: It's a 550 pound eight foot marble free form coffee table.

DLVRY MAN: You're telling me? I mean what's it supposed to be?

LIZ: It's done in the shape of Dore Schary.

DLVRY MAN: (Studying table) I can't see it. It looks more like a quick-frozen Darryl Zanuck to me.

LIZ: It's Schary! I designed it, you fool! (Picking up a large splinter of glass and chopping at her hair, hit or miss fashion.) I cut my own hair, you know.

DLVRY MAN: (Squinting at table) Dore Schary eh?

MIKIE: (On phone in other room) Buy a thousand shares of Davey Crockett.

MAID: The apples are picked.

LIZ: Well, get that pie baked. Silver Screen will be here at three to take pictures of me taking it out of the oven.

MAID: What an old fashioned mother you are.

(Front door opens, but dramatic beige neon lights fail to operate, as Mikie has pulled plug. Liz moves snail-like to greet husband who stands in doorway. 45 minutes later, she reaches him.

MICHAEL: I'm home. (They embrace)

LIZ: You're wet.

MICHAEL: I fell in the pool.

LIZ: What did you bring me?

MICHAEL: The Hope Diamond.

LIZ: (Squealing) OOOOOH! I got it after all! (He tosses it to her and scales the tree.) I've been thinking it over. That table does look like Zanuck. Take it back.

(Deliveryman turns pale at prospect and steadies himself against drapes causing Hi-Fi to start up. Michael, (hearing applause) comes out of tree-house to take bow and plummets to floor.

LIZ: I'm so tired. I think I'll tell the studio I'll do only one picture a year from now on.

MIKIE: (Toddling into room) You'll do three and like it. You're working for me now.

LIZ: WHAT?

MIKIE: (Smugly) I just bought control of Loews, Inc.

LIZ: What a naughty thing to do. I'll have to spank you.

MIKIE: Lay one finger on me and you're on suspension. (He leaves playing catch with Hope Diamond)

LIZ: But . . . (She turns desperately to husband who is no fool. He has painted himself beige, and disappeared into the motif.)

MAID: Silver Screen is here.

(Liz wearily puts plug back into socket, causing beige neon lights to flicker on about the dramatic living room, made even more dramatic by the shadow of the deliveryman who has hung himself from the tree.)

THE END

HEADACHE? COLD MISERY?
Why wait for old-fashioned cold relief? Go Kill yourself!

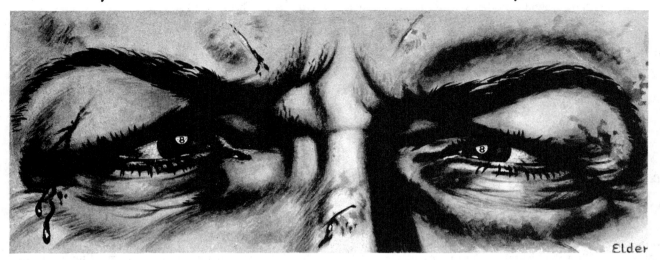

GET FASTER PAIN RELIEF WITH
BOFFORIN
Acts twice as fast

Won't upset your gaskets!

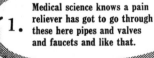

1. Medical science knows a pain reliever has got to go through these here pipes and valves and faucets and like that.

2. Bofforin gets through these things <u>twice as fast</u> and the reason <u>why</u> is that Bofforin combines axle-grease with a tested, proven rust solvent.

3. That way the pain reliever gets into the blood stream and once it reaches the blood stream... Boffo! Bofforin acts <u>twice as fast</u>!

4. And all your motors and pumps will go humming along like a sewing machine. You'll work wonders with a "button-hole stitcher" atttched to your nose.

Ask your own doctor about how Bofforin acts... how when it goes around in those pumps like in our diagram and how it goes up through them pipes to them switchboards and lights up the little lights and rings the little bells, and switches the little switches and turns the little dials (they tell you which way is North), I'll bet you never knew you had such little lights and dials and switches in your head.

Ask your own doctor about how Bofforin acts inside those pipes and valves. Better still, ask your own plumber.

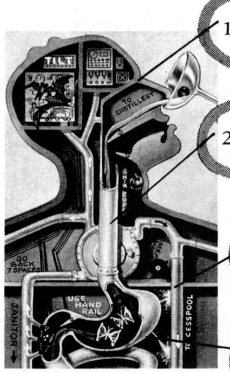

ASK YOUR PLUMBER ABOUT BOFFORIN

NOTE: THOUSANDS have switched from rust preventer to BOFFORIN.

MOVIE DEPT. PART III

Now, in competition with cheapskate imitation MAD magazines, we announce bargain value! Two, for price of one! A second movie review! A review of...

the seven itchy years

PICTURES BY WILL ELDER

Famous picture of Marilyn Marone being caught by gust of wind from subway grating with fascinating results in "The Seven Itchy Years."

PICTURE OF EDITORS going into theatre to see preview of "The Seven Itchy Years."

CONTINUED ON NEXT PAGE

YOU'LL WATCH THE STORY UNFOLD IN AUTHENTIC NEW YORK APARTMENT

YOU'LL ENJOY WATCHING LEAD MAN THOMAS EAWRL, SEEN ON RIGHT

WATCHING VICTOR MOO AS THE PLUMBER (LOWER LEFT), IS A HOWL

ROBERT ANIMAL (ABOVE) SUNNY TUFFY (BELOW) ARE FUN TO WATCH

"The Seven Itchy Years" is a catchy title that should perhaps be explained before we go any farther.

You see... when a man is married for seven years and the only woman he is familiar with is his wife... he may sometimes see a pretty girl and all of a sudden get very itchy. To put it very simply... the seven year itch is this:

Ring worm.

Some types of ring worm rashes have been known to incubate for seven year periods and longer.

To get on with our story... originally "The Seven Itchy Years" was produced as a play on Broadway. Comparing the play to the movie, there were very marked differences. Very marked.

The play's admission price was higher, for one thing. Then they didn't have air-conditioning in the play theatre.

And the play was itchier.

Much itchier.

Let it suffice to say that you will enjoy watching Marilyn Marone, Thomas Eawrl, Marilyn Marone, Sunny Tuffy, Marilyn Marone and others in this picture which is photographed in flawless cinemascopic technicolor with stereophonic sound which made it seem that the sound was coming from all directions... In front of us... from the side of us... and in back of us.

Imagine our surprise when we discovered the sound really *was* coming from in back of us...

This bum in the next row talking out loud to his wife through the *whole* picture.

END

PICTURE OF EDITORS swarming out of theatre after seeing "The Seven Itchy Years."

EDUCATION DEPT.

THE FOLLOWING HAS BEEN PAINSTAKINGLY PREPARED BY OUR FAR RANGING RESEARCH AND SURVEY STAFF FROM A MULTITUDE OF CAREFULLY ORGANIZED FACTS HE HAS COLLECTED IN HIS COMPOSITION BOOK FOR THIS ARTICLE:

HOW TO BE SMART

ontrary to our usual policy and all kidding aside, this is going to be a very serious and useful article.

All kidding aside.

Now many people are under the impression that the world is a pretty dumb place and there aren't many smart people around nowadays. To foolishly say whether there *are* lot's of those dumb people will not be the purpose of this article.

To *help* all those millions of dumb people will be the purpose of this article.

And with smartness in the minority, let's face it...you are probably one of 'those'...

Especially since you're reading this magazine.

However, cheer up. You too can be smart. It's easy.

For instance, what makes a person smart? Is it because you *think* you're smart?

Naaah!

Everyone thinks they're smart. ...don't mean a thing.

What makes you smart is when *other* people think you're smart... when they see you passing and say, 'He look smart.' and throw rocks.

The point is...it's how you *look* that makes you smart.

That's where we come in.

On the following pages we will show you in a matter of minutes, how you can look and act so that everyone will think you are smart, making you, in effect, smart.

"Make me smart in a matter of minutes?" you say, "ridiculous!"

See, we say, you are getting smart already.

PICTURES BY WALLACE WOOD　　CONTINUED ON NEXT PAGE

how to look smart

What a college education accomplishes in years, a well-chosen adornment can do in minutes...

if a loutish look is yours, the condition can be reversed by plain use of heavy black eyeglasses. (glass not necessary.)   with heavy black eyeglasses, loutish looking clod becomes intelligent looking clod.

you can rise above all the other scrub-women with a simple device.   a slender nickel-plate cigarette holder whipped out at the coffee-break will give you that smart look.

don't be ordinary, (a sure sign of feeble-mindedness). like for instance, don't wear ordinary cuff-links.   wear cuff-links made out of out of old coffee grinders.

if you have the ignoramus look of the rest of the pool-hall crowd, an intelligent gleam is yours for the taking.   grow a well-trimmed beard. it will get you out of that pool-hall class ...it will get you out of that pool-hall. they'll never let you back in.

Odd clothing, a strange textured jacket, cleverly fastened drop seat, create smart impressions.

just think when you enter the cocktail party, how smart you'll look...

with your fluorescent pink weskit, hand-woven wood-pulp skirt, etc.

or else, you're back outside elegant party and this time you come in...

with faded dungarees, surplus army sweat-shirts and basketball shoes!

or else, you're back outside, and now you create biggest impression of all.

you come in *naked*.

how to act smart

Sitting is important in standing out. Outstanding sitting will sit you in good standing . . . er avoid chairs. fling yourself down upon the floor in a gracefully flung posture

there is nothing as smart looking as a flinged figure that is gracefully flung

Cultivate a withering sneer.
practice this sneer. try it on your friends.

Say didja listen to Eddie Fishie's latest 'pop' record, huh? didja? didja huh? didja?

Carefully chosen words make meaningless conversation, intelligent meaningless conversation.

'fantastic' is a high-class smart word. if your boy-friend wiggles his ears,
don't say: ...say:

'fabulous' is good. when your neighbor's son shows you his frog collection,
don't say: ...say:

it's smart to use the word 'darling' whether at the cocktail party or the meat market,
don't say: ...say:

how to live smart

Smartness is accented by strange objects in your home, both mineral, vegetable and people.

fireplace designed like bonfire on floor.

a painting...the harder to understand the better.

strange light fixture not to be confused with mobile.

automatic record player automatically smashes pop records.

arty coffee table converted from Zuñi gravestone.

chair, made from rare gnu leather.

TO SUM IT ALL UP...to be smart, *be different*. If the others order peanut butter sandwiches, you ask for Pizza. If everyone stands on line, you sneak around the other way. If they talk about the U.S., you tell them about Paris. If they happen to be worldly, you tell them you're a Martian. Yes, you will be very impressive if you can tell them you're a Martian.

Finally...if after reading this article, you are satisfied to remain amongst the peasants, don't go making fun of every person who *is* different or

How to be Smart

strange mobile not to be confused with light fixture.

strange person not to be confused with anything.

interesting shape. ...no, not the girl!

chair designed to grip you.

plenty books (you don't have to read 'em)

hors d'oeuvres of pickled tentacle tips, smoked african beetle grubs.

acts like a Martian... ...he *might really be* a Martian!

SPORTS DEPT. PART II

MY SECRET

Benn Ogen reveals mystery gimmick that made him rich and famous

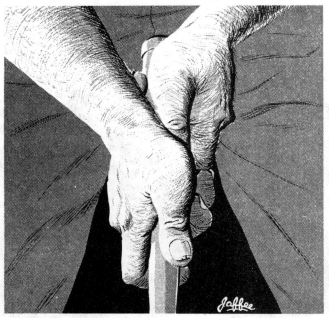

WITHOUT SECRET Ogen's conventional grip is exactly the same one he has used for years with unspectacular results.

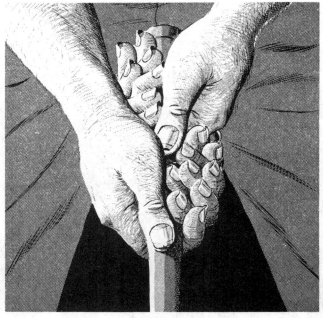

WITH SECRET Ogen shifts his fingers ever so slightly which is the main reason why his opponents could not detect it.

by BENN OGEN
PICTURES BY AL JAFFEE

The better golfer you become the more trouble you'll have with the hook. A hook is the natural outgrowth of a more powerful swing. It'd be almost funny if it weren't so pathetic to see the ridiculous lengths that some famous tournament players have gone to to get rid of this terrible problem. Take the case of my old friend Sam Snood. Sam approached the problem with calm logic. He figured that since a hook veers off to the left he could solve it by standing a little further over to the right. Little by little he edged further and further over to the right and when the ball was almost landing just right he suddenly developed a terrible slice. Since a slice veers off in the opposite direction of a hook, poor old Sam could do nothing else but start working his way back in the other direction. Just as the slice was about to disappear guess what? . . . that's right . . . the hook returned and with calm logic Sam proceeded to smash every club over his caddie's head. Mang Lloydrum tried various methods of licking the demon hook including a special set of anti-hook clubs with built in battery-operated swivel heads. A mid-game short circuit ended that idea. Alfred E. Neuman tried the most audacious experiment of all . . . he gave up golf. Oh these poor, poor deluded boys. I just couldn't help chuckling to myself as I watched their pitiful efforts when all the while (chuckle chuckle) I had the *real* secret. Boy, I just hated myself for laughing at their (HA, HA) expense, but with my secret I was (HO, HO) beating the pants off 'em. They were (HOO, HAH-HA) starving. But now that I'm load—er—now that I've decided to retire I'd like to share my secret with them.

What makes the whole thing so very interesting is the utter simplicity of my secret. I can't understand why no one ever noticed it. You start by simply gripping your club in the usual manner . . . then with a simple motion you start to pronate the right hand till a small "V" is formed between the wrists. Apply the rule about isosceles triangles to this "V" then go on to figure out the distance from angle "A" to angle "B." If it exceeds 11½ degrees, compensate with a simple reverse pronation until left thumb comes right under the middle knuckle of left forefinger. Simple, hey? But wait—that's not the secret yet. You will notice that after all this maneuvering that there's no place to put the right pinky. Well, just point it towards where you'd like the ball to go, then try to hit the ball there. If it happens—man! *You've* got the *secret!*

"Tricky lil' Devil, ain't I?"

you read it in MAD

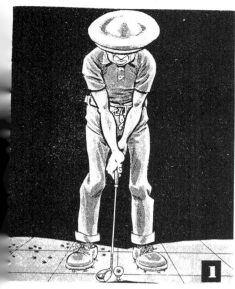

THE SECRET BEGINS when Ogen goes into his backswing. He starts his

loosening up as shown in picture 2 and continues until he reaches critical moment. (3)

Whereupon his left hand pronates downwards (4) with great speed (5)

SECRET CONCLUDES with reverse pronation upwards (see 6) and a firm

tightening grip (7) Downswing continues till the moment of contact (as in 8) resulting in

follow-thru and right pinky pointing to spot ball should light (9)

Why settle for others when Beauty

INSIDE SECRET OF HEALTHIER REST!

"PLAIN ORDINARY" MATTRESS

With springs wired together, one spring pulls down the next as shown by spilling contents of glass

BEAUTYDREAMY MATTRESS

With independent springs, one spring can't pull next spring down. Contents of glass do not spill out.

Exclusive Beautydreamy independent springs support each glass independently. Beautydreamy support springs are free to push back. Push down . . . Beautydreamy pushes back. Push down hard . . . Beautydreamy knocks you head over teakettle.

Many people test a mattress by pressing down with thei hands. But this way can fool you. The only way to test mattress is to lie down on it full length with glasses o liquid all around you. Then you've got to spring to you feet and leap rapidly all over the mattress in between th

A mattress can be too firm. Lie on the floo and see. If your present mattress feels har der than that floor, check the mattress care fully. It may be a pool table.

Plenty people are

by keeping plenty glasse

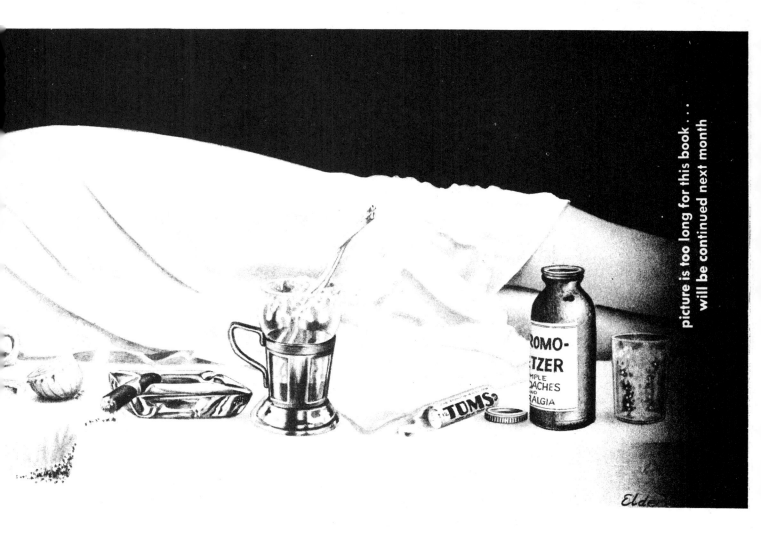

picture is too long for this book.... will be continued next month

dreamy balances drinking glasses!

glasses, making sure to bring your heels down smartly and with great force. Wear baseball shoes. Once you do this and find how you get sopping wet on other mattresses you will know that Beautydreamy is for you. For Beautydreamy has an exclusive secret: Each spring is separate, giving each part of your body and each drinking glass separate support. You can buy your Beautydreamy with separate spring construction either a separate spring at a time or you can buy enough separate springs to make up a whole Beautydreamy mattress equipped bed.

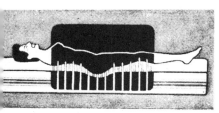

mattress can be too thin. X-ray would ow your weight supported by box spring. -ray would also show plenty more so watch t for that beady-eyed X-ray operator.

Beautydreamy—firm enough for a 250 pounder! Springs won't break under a 65,000 pound truck! Buy a Beautydreamy to put in your garage for your 65,000 pound truck!

Beautydreamy—comfortable enough for a child! Beautydreamy combines gentleness needed for satisfying rest and firmness needed for devastating broad jumps into bed.

getting healthier rest on Beautydreamy tonight.

f fruit juice, milk, etc., on that separate spring construction.

THIS FEATURE TELEVISION ED

ED SUVILLAN AT WORK with his show of shows, showing his qualities that characterize him... a pulsating energy combined with zealous and spirited activity and a frenzied devotion to dynamic, vigorous action with an agility and intense enthusiasm... and mainly, he hardly moves.

You read it in MAD

TV DEPT.

...ABOUT THE BIGGEST THING ON YOUR ...ET. NO...NOT THE INDOOR ANTENNA! THE...

SUVILLAN SHOW

Since this article is intended to give you an idea of how the highly successful Ed Suvillan Show goes ... to those of you who aren't acquainted with and haven't seen the Ed Suvillan Show, this article is for you. In other words, this article is good for about three people. Everybody else turn to next article. Anyhow, on the following pages are samples of the unbelievable array of variety and talent from all over the world that appears on the Ed Suvillan Show. Some of the acts are new and some have been seen before. Some have even been repeated on the Show by popular request. As a matter of fact you know one performer who has been on the Ed Suvillan Show countless times and who returns to the Show again and again:

Ed Suvillan.

CONTINUED ON NEXT PAGE

PICTURES BY WILL ELDER

POPULAR NOTION THAT SUVILLAN IS EXPRESSIONLESS IS DISPROVED BY CANDID VIEWS OF SUVILLAN'S DRAMATIC EYE MOVEMENTS

FURTHER DISPROOF OF THE ED. SUVILLAN STONEFACE IS DRAMATICALLY CAPTURED AS HE MOMENTARILY TWITCHES LIPS PURSED

"EXPRESSIONLESS" MYTH IS SWEPT AWAY AS SUVILLAN, IN BURST OF EMOTION RUBS HANDS AND PURSES LIPS AT THE SAME TIME

remember! April 1956

Ed Suvillan

Ed Suvillan features vaudeville acts ... the finest ventriloquists and smartest dummies in very tricky acts like as follows.

Ed Suvillan

Suvillan spares no expense in searching for interesting acts, not only at home but all over the world.

Show is so star studded... even audience is famous and at some point Suvillan asks well-known personalities to stand up.

Ed Suvillan

Suvillan is a good sport, being very often the butt of jokes and parodies on own show and taking it like a good sport.

At a Special Term, Part III of the

Supreme Court of the State ***

PRESENT:

    HON. ALFRED E. NEUMAN,

                  Justice.

------------------------------x

ED SUVILLAN,

                  Plaintiff,

       -against-

MAD MAGAZINE,

                  Defendant.

------------------------------x

    Upon reading and filing the summons and verified complaint herein and the sworn affidavit of ED SUVILLAN, ***
    LET the defendant above named show cause before this Court, at a Special Term, Part III thereof, ***
WHY the defendant should not be permanently restrained and enjoined from publishing, printing, circulating, selling and distributing copies of a certain magazine entitled "MAD" containing an article of and concerning the plaintiff, which article, *** unlawfully holds him up to public scorn and ridicule, vilifies and defames his name and character, and otherwise injures his reputation and credit; and sufficient cause appearing, it is hereby
    ORDERED, that pending the hearing and final determination of this motion, the defendant is hereby stayed from publishing, printing, and circulating copies of the aforesaid magazine entitled "MAD" containing the aforesaid article complained of; ***

Alfred E. Neuman
JUSTICE OF THE SUPREME COURT

all kidding aside, he really is a good sport.

HOLLYWOOD DEPT.
SCENES WE'D LIKE TO SEE
The Fighter Who Didn't Rally.

"Alice is here, and your mother forgives you."

You read it in MAD

HOBBIES DEPT.

STAMPS

COLLECTING IS POPULAR WORLD WIDE HOBBY

PICTURES BY AL JAFFEE

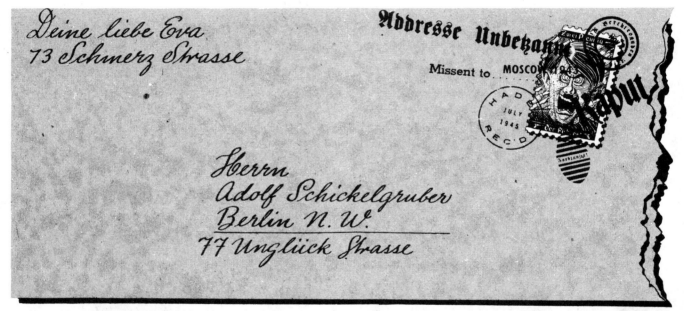

WORLD'S MOST WORTHLESS STAMP (EVEN THOUGH A RARITY) BECAUSE OF ITS VERY POOR CONDITION

The rarity and condition of a stamp determines its worth. To illustrate our point we decided to contact the owner of the world's most valuable stamp... the two cent blue Queen Zamba. After months of negotiation we were finally permitted to photograph this breathtaking beauty. Unfortunately, however, while setting up our cameras we somehow misplaced it.

The stamp on the envelope above will illustrate our point just as well. It shows the many damages that detract from any stamp's value.

Stamps fall into many fascinating categories. On the next page we have printed some unusual selections which are sure to draw even the most hardbitten skeptic into the wonderful world of philately.

UNUSUAL ERRORS MAKE STAMPS COLLECTOR'S ITEMS

you read it in MAD

COMMEMORATIVE

Some stamps are issued to commemorate important events in the history of a country. To the right is an outstanding example of this produced by one of our South American neighbors. This attractive three stamp series tells the story of the reign of the country's most recent ruler. Each stamp was released with timely significance on the dates indicated.

February 14

February 17

February 19

GOOFS—ACCIDENTAL

Carelessness somewhere along the stamp production line often creates extremely valuable items. These are usually rare because as soon as the postal authorities discover their errors they correct them. Common examples are:
A) Imprint on paper, forgetting perforations.
B) Perforations on paper, forgetting imprint.
C) Perforations and imprint, forgetting paper.

A.   B.   C.

GOOFS—INTENTIONAL

Since mistakes make stamps valuable it follows that unscrupulous persons would try to exploit the situation. This has brought forth, the "legitimate counterfeit" stamp. It is created by an unprincipled printing and engraving employee who tampers with plates, pulls proofs, fixes plates right again, and sneaks the bogus proofs out for a profitable sale.

real.....3¢

phony....$1400.00

PRIZED RARITIES

Hand printed stamps are rarest of all, like one at right made by an early Hawaiian missionary. He engraved design on a smooth rock and inked it with vegetable dyes. Then while holding a piece of paper with his left thumb on a flat rock on the ground, he brought the inked rock swiftly down removing his thumb at the last second. He only made one of these.

priceless, hand printed

SPECIAL PURPOSE

Most people think of stamps in relation to mail service only. While it's true that most of them are produced for that purpose there are still many millions made for other reasons. Even within the postal service itself there are different types such as special delivery, postage due, pony express, Zeppelin air mail, late delivery, damaged delivery, no delivery, etc. . . .

for licenses

for subs

INSTRUCTIONS: To you grownups... Here at the end of our magazine, now that your whole attitude towards life has shifted as a result of reading the past fifty-five pages... what could be more appropriate than paper dolls for you to cut out. You might try pasting Pete and Pat onto a sheet of cardboard for stiffness, before cutting them out. You might even paste them onto a thin sheet of plywood for real stiffness and cut them out with a coping saw. Then again, a sheet of tempered steel, trimmed with a gas torch would make the ideal backing.

PICTURES BY WILL ELDER

Watch for our next issue. Perhaps we will then show you how to play the interesting game called FLAP THE LOWER LIP, another MAD time and mind killer.

GAME DEPT.

GRINGO

Mr. Ernie Kovacs, foremost GRINGO player is shown in the process of shouting "Gringo!" three times, as his "roundee" lands in the "High Roller Bonus" square.

GRINGO, which Mr. Kovacs himself introduced to the Western Hemisphere, promises to be the hottest parlor game since Monopoly, Scrabble and Lotto.

On our right is the directions sheet extracted from a set of GRINGO. A careful reading will give you a clear idea of what the game is all about ... and what will be plainer still is if you had one grunch but the egg-plant over there.

PICTURES BY WILL ELDER

DIRECTIONS
© ERNIE KOVACS

IN EACH BOX
- 27 Small red squares which are called **Enchiladoes**
- 13 Blue, plastic triangles called **Blue, plastic triangles**
- 17 Perforated disks, called "**Roundees**"
- 113 Yellow darts
- 113 Green darts
- 113 White darts
- 2 Orange darts
- 1 Deck of playing cards with pictures of former mayors of Hong Kong from the **Ming Dynasty** to the present era
- 1 Large **GRINGO** board with automatic lazy susan

HOW TO PLAY
Any number of players may play **GRINGO** ... two, three, four, seven, eleven, thirteen, one hundred and forty-four ... whole towns have been known to play.

TO START THE GAME
The player who rolls the **highest number** on the eleven pairs of dice goes **First**, he rolls the same dice (with the exception of the one pair

1 Player **A** puts roundees, triangles, and enchiladoes on board. Dice roll is 2 points, **A** loses turn.

FOR PLAYING GRINGO

marked **High Roller First**. As this pair is only included in determining who is first.) After totalling his score on PENCIL and PAPER, he takes an **Enchilado** and moves it the corresponding number of squares on the **Gringo** board. He then rolls again, this time the pair of dice marked **High Roller First** may be included if his **Enchilado** landed on the square marked HIGH ROLLER BONUS.

ROUNDEE MOVE

On this roll he moves his BLUE, plastic triangle according to his total and moves a **Roundee** (The Perforated Tile Disk) two and a half times one quarter the distance the total of the distance of the **Enchilado** and the **Blue, Plastic Triangle**, unless the player on his RIGHT throws a Green dart in the air, shouting **GRINGO** three times, in which case player number one must move the **Enchilado** and the **Roundee** four times the cube root of the sum he throws, this is a special throw, on the dice marked HIGH ROLLER FIRST.

THIRD GRINGO RULE

He then moves his Roundee correspondingly, unless the Green dart thrown by the player to his RIGHT landed before the third **GRINGO**. If the Green dart landed on the SECOND **GRINGO**, player number one moves his **Roundee** ONE QUARTER way round the board PROVIDED the player to his LEFT does not call out the name of one of the **Hong Kong Mayors** as he throws a YELLOW dart into the air on the first **GRINGO** shouted by the player to the RIGHT of the first player.

FREE THROW

This is standard procedure on first roll with ONE EXCEPTION: if the name of the **Hong Kong Mayor** called out by the player to the LEFT with the yellow dart starts with the letter "B," then, all must **roll again** and move their **Roundees** BACK **two spaces**, unless of course, their Blue, plastic markers are on a square marked **Omit Hong Kong Mayor "B" penalty**, in which case, the player whose Blue, plastic marker is on this **Omit Hong Kong Mayor "B" penalty square** gets a **free throw** with a white dart, eliminating ANY player from the game he happens to hit.

EXAMPLES OF GRINGO MOVES

Players represented by A, B, C, D.

2 Meanwhile, **B** pulls out with **A**'s roundees, triangles and enchiladoes and is thus eliminated by **A**.

3 **C** and **D** roll straight sevens winning all of **A**'s roundees, etc. However, **A** eliminates **C** and **D**.

Where can you buy "Sun Pictures"?

RAISED PINKY DEPT.

This next informative article is directed primarily at clods who got no table manners... which means practically everyone will be interested in this informative article, mainly because practically everyone who reads MAD is obviously a clod. To teach you correct table manners, we have called upon an ex-clod (he's no longer a clod since Life magazine accepted his work), Basil Wolverton. Here's your chance, then to learn table manners by attempting to answer the following...

Dining Etiquette
QUIZ

QUESTION: WHICH IS THE ACCEPTABLE MANNER OF EATING PEAS, (A) OR (B)?

ANSWER: (A) BY ALL MEANS. JUST BE SURE KNIFE IS MAGNETIZED AND PEAS ARE COOKED IN IRON FILINGS. FORMERLY USED FUNNEL METHOD BECAME SOCIALLY TABOO AFTER THE DAY ALFRED E. NEUMAN SWALLOWED ONE.

QUESTION: WHICH IS THE PROPER MANNER FOR DISPOSING OF SCRAPS, (A) OR (B)?

ANSWER: SCRAPS THROWN ON FLOOR CAN CAUSE WAITER TO SLIP WHILE BRINGING DESSERT. PROPER MANNER, SHOWN IN (B) IS TO SHOVE SCRAPS INSIDE SHIRT. YOU MAY GET A GREASY ABDOMEN BUT YOU'LL SAVE ON NEXT MEAL.

QUESTION: WHAT SHOULD BE DONE WITH YOUR LONG BEARD WHILE EATING?

ANSWER: NEVER BE INCONSIDERATE LIKE BEWHISKERED CLOD SHOWN IN (B). PROPER PLACE FOR BEARD IS IN OWN PLATE. ALSO, YOU MAY BE ABLE TO CON AN EXTRA SERVING BY COMPLAINING OF A HAIR IN YOUR FOOD.

QUESTION: IF YOU MUST, WHICH IS THE PROPER WAY TO LEAN ON ONE'S ELBOW AT TABLE?

ANSWER: THOUGH MAYONNAISE-DRENCHED LEAFY SALAD IS SOOTHING AND COOLING, SCALDING HOT COFFEE WILL GET ELBOW CLEANER. THEREFORE, IF YOU MUST LEAN ELBOW ON TABLE WHILE EATING, (A) IS PREFERABLE.

QUESTION: WHICH IS THE DESIRABLE METHOD OF OBTAINING FOOD WITHOUT ASKING FOR IT?

ANSWER: IF YOU DESIRE A PARTICULAR DISH, PULLING IT TO YOU WITH TABLECLOTH AS IN (B) IS EASIER AND MORE DESIRABLE. REACHING FOR GRUNCH WHEN EGGPLANT IS OVER THERE MAY RESULT IN YOUR STRAINING TENDON.

UNSUNG HEROES DEPT.

It isn't every day that somebody goes up in an Aerobee rocket. Bet nobody on your block ever went up in an Aerobee rocket. We asked Caesar, the elevator operator in the MAD *Building, who goes up plenty, and even he never went up in an Aerobee rocket. So when somebody goes up in an Aerobee rocket, we figure he's pretty much a hero. We figure he pretty much deserves our country's thanks. But when we looked into it, by George, we were pretty much shocked. Seems nobody bothered to give our country's thanks to ...*

FREE FALL FERRIS

PROPOSED STATUE honoring F. F. Ferris, to be erected at site of momentous ascent. Aspirin bottle pedestal symbolizes sacrifice Ferris made for country. As a result of heroic act, Ferris now suffers from headaches ...

UNSUNG HERO Ferris before induction into Air Force. A healthy, active specimen of young American Rodenthood.

UNSUNG HERO Ferris upon discharge from Air Force... a complete physical wreck. See A.F. medical report (below)

```
OFFICIAL MEDICAL RELEASE
Halloman Air Force Base
Alamogordo, New Mexico
Reference:   FERRIS, F.F.  (M-098-897-876)
             Attached to Air Research and Development
             Command, U.S.A.F. Project 3456789-a
Recommendation: IMMEDIATE DISCHARGE
Findings of Medical Board:
  Subject, involved in recent flight 200,000 feet in-
to upper stratosphere, was recovered alive and in
apparent good health. However, because of rigors of
flight, symptoms soon developed, including marked he-
matoma of semi-circular canal of middle-ear apparatus,
disturbing subject's equilibrium; frequent migraine
headaches; recurring nosebleeds; ingrown toenail.
PROGNOSIS: poor. Advisable subject be given immediate
medical discharge, mainly because this rodent is sick.
Appropriate steps should be taken to separate subject,
```

(ABOVE) Copy of top secret official Air Force medical report lists terrible results of F. F. Ferris' thankless flight in experimental Aerobee rocket.

(BELOW) Chart clearly shows how rocket take-off acceleration exerts tremendous force of 15Gs which in turn causes blood to settle in body extremities.

EXPECTED NORMAL REACTION

UNEXPECTED FERRIS REACTION

IT WASN'T THAT F. F. Ferris minded so much being inducted into the Air Force. It was just that he'd had his little heart set on the Navy, his forebears all being loyal Navy men. Documentary evidence indicates that not one of Ferris' navy ancestors ever left a sinking ship. Ferris' great-grandfather, for example, is still aboard the ironclad *Monitor*. Since *Monitor* sank in 1863, Grandpa stays put. Ferris, speedily inducted, received his instructions immediately upon arriving at the Air Force Research and Development Command. He was to make the ascent that very same day, without benefit of pre-flight schooling, without benefit of Link-trainer instruction, and without benefit of a visit to the P.X. Two monkeys would accompany him on historic stratospheric flight. But at the last moment, the monkeys chickened out and had to be anaesthetized.

PICTURES BY WALLACE WOOD

FERRIS IS SNAPPED UP BY AIR FORCE FOR DANGEROUS MISSION

FERRIS' RELATIVES ALL ATTEND HISTORIC AEROBEE LAUNCHING

CUT-AWAY VIEW OF AEROBEE CLEARLY SHOWS RESTRAINED MONKEYS AND UNRESTRAINED FERRIS IN SEPARATE COMPARTMENTS

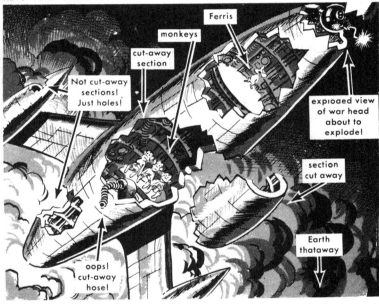

DURING INITIAL ACCELERATION AT TAKE-OFF OF AEROBEE ROCKET, FERRIS IS SUBJECTED TO GRAVITY FORCE FIFTEEN TIMES HIS OWN WEIGHT. PICTURES BELOW SHOW CONTORTED EXPRESSIONS ON FERRIS' FACE AS HE ANTICIPATES FORCE WHILE WAITING FOR TAKE-OFF.

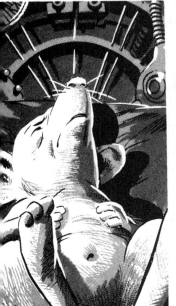   

FREE FALL FERRIS CONTINUED

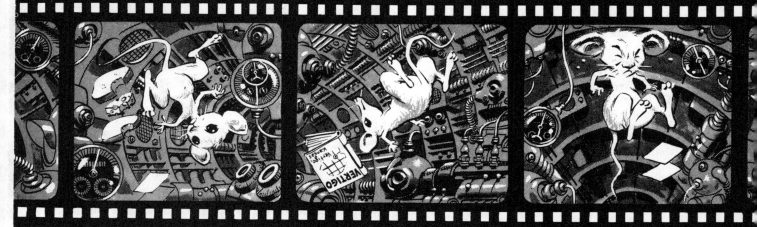

FILM STRIP (enlarged above) was made just as Aerobee rocket attained maximum height of trajectory. In first frame (left), F. F. Ferris is submitted to a state of weightlessness, or zero gravity, in second frame (center), he floats free within his compartment, unable to control his movements normally, having lost sense of direction, orientation. In third frame (right), zero gravity has Ferris falling up. Fourth frame, (not shown) has Ferris throwing up . . .

At mathematically calculated zenith of flight, trigger mechanism releases compartment containing Ferris and valuable instruments used to record psychological and physiological reactions of subjects. Those scientists, they think of everything. Those scientists, they got dandy slide-rules. Those scientists! Boy! They forgot about ditching the monkeys!

This, then, is our plea for recognition of Free Fall Ferris and his valiant, patriotic sacrifice for his country, above and beyond the call of duty. Fifty miles above and beyond! The President might have cited Ferris personally but the Mouse-Trap Trust had too strong a Washington lobby.

So if you see F. F. Ferris staggering and weaving down your street, please be kind. He is not drunk, just plain stratosphere-happy. Remember, when you see him, that he is an unsung hero. Remember to write your congressman, requesting a monthly 100% total disability check for this red-blooded rodent whose services helped make the Air Force space-wise. Remember to say that you read it in MAD. Then remember to get out of town! END

Where are they hiding the Trylon and Perisphere?

ADVICE DEPT. PART I
ALFRED E. NEUMAN ANSWERS YOUR QUESTIONS

PROBLEM:

Two weeks ago, I was laid off my job . . .

I came home to find my wife in the arms of another man . . .

As I stumbled from the house, I saw my children being carried away by some fiend . . .

On the way to summon the police, I was beaten and robbed . . .

I am cold, hungry and thoroughly depressed. I sometimes say to myself, "If I knew how to tie a hangman's knot, I would end it all!" What should I do?—Anxious

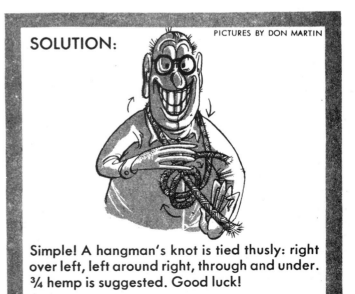

SOLUTION:

PICTURES BY DON MARTIN

Simple! A hangman's knot is tied thusly: right over left, left around right, through and under. ¾ hemp is suggested. Good luck!

you read it in MAD   Why not revive "Flat Foot Floogie"?

MASS HYSTERIA DEPT.

With this article MAD takes another step in its insidious campaign of examining, evaluating, and then destroying culture in general by turning its attention to the interesting and baffling phenomenon of...

Gasping, shouting, and shrieking, audience of teen-agers leap from seats, dance in aisles, and stampede toward stage moment Elvis Pelvis strums electric guitar and begins to sing. Shrieking, dancing and stampeding reaction is due to teen-agers' sudden shocked discovery that electricity wired into Elvis's guitar is also wired into the audience seats.

FACIAL EXPRESSIONS DISPLAY GAMUT OF EMOTION

SAD LAMENT

PELVIS EXPOUNDS SAD LAMENT of the latest hit, "Standing By The Coroner."

PLAINTIVE SOB

PELVIS WAILS PLAINTIVE SOB of popular "On the Street Where You Lie."

WORRIED MOAN

PELVIS CHOKES WORRIED MOAN of the torch song, "I Almost Found My Mind."

ELVIS PELVIS

In the music business, it seems that Perry Como, with his relaxed and flaccid style of singing, makes new friends and wins new plaudits each time he makes an appearance.

On the other hand, it seems that Elvis Pelvis, with his frenzied shake, wriggle, squirm, rock and roll style of howling, makes new enemies and incites new objections each time he makes an appearance.

Since this kind of reaction is familiar to us (the same thing seems to happen in the magazine business each time MAD makes an appearance), your Editors attended a performance of said teen-age idol in order to see what gives.

What gives, we observed, is Elvis's pelvis.

Candid pictures of Elvis, one-time hillbilly singer, show sensuous motions which punctuate sensuous lament. Sensuous motions and lament are caused by sentimental holdover from hillbilly days. Elvis still wears itchy flannel longjohns.

ELVIS PELVIS SINGS VARIOUS TYPES OF POP TUNES

CAREFREE CHUCKLE

PELVIS LILTS CAREFREE CHUCKLE of the catchy "It Only Hurts When I Laugh!"

HAPPY GIGGLE

PELVIS CROONS HAPPY GIGGLE of the amusing ballad, "Electrocution Day."

HYSTERICAL HOWL

PELVIS BELLOWS HYSTERICAL HOWL of revived "My Old Kentucky Home Brew."

** There will probably never be another Yankee center fielder named Joe DiMaggio.

SPORTS DEPT.

Where are those nice loving couples you used to see in the park each evening, walking hand-in-hand or smooching?

What's happened to those nice friendly folks you used to see in their homes every evening, playing bridge or poker? Hah?

Where are those tough-looking teenagers you used to see on the street corners each evening, getting in trouble? Hah?

Oops! They're still there!

PICTURES BY JACK DAVIS

Well anyway, what about the rest of the people? Where are they these evenings? Here's where they are! Indulging in the sport that enables them to unleash all their pent-up hostilities!

Yes, this is it! If you've got any pent-up hostilities, this is the sport that enables you to unleash them. And if you haven't got any pent-up hostilities, this is the sport that enables you to get some plenty quick. Just pick up one of those sixteen-pound balls (if you can), imagine that those ten pins down there some sixty-odd feet away are your ten worst enemies, and *let 'em have it!* What a thrill! Just listen to the rumble as the ball thunders down the alley! Just listen to the deafening roar as the ball collides with wood! Just listen to the splintering crash as the pins fly in all directions! Just listen to the blood-curdling shriek as the pinboy gets hit in the head! By George, what a thrill! By George, it makes you feel good! By George, so that's why, these evenings, everybody with pent-up hostilities is...

BOWLING

CLOSE-UPS OF BOWLER SHOW RELEASE OF PENT-UP EMOTION

eaves hand... Spins down alley... Hooks in sharply... Approaches pins... .... A STRIKE!

DIAGRAMS BELOW SHOW TYPES OF THROWS USED IN BOWLING

THE STRAIGHT BALL   THE HOOK BALL   THE CURVE BALL   THE LOFT BALL

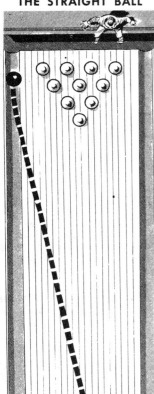 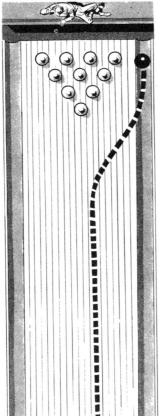 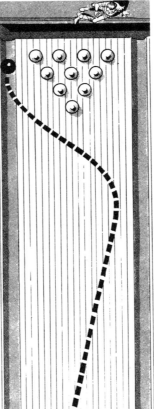 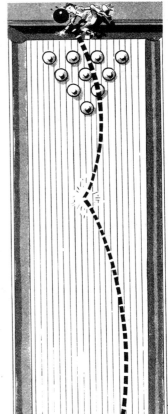

There is never any doubt when you use the straight ball delivery. Just as soon as you release the ball, it heads straight for the gutter!

The hook ball delivery fools you at first. Just before it's about to smash into the pins, it takes a quick spin and hooks right into the gutter!

The curve ball fools you even more! It looks like it's headed for the right gutter, but then it reverses path and lands in the opposite gutter!

The loft ball delivery fools the *pinboy* by striking midway down the alley, lofting over the pins, and knocking him square into the gutter!

** We feel slighted when a bus-driver tells us to move to the rear of the bus when it's empty.

BOWLING CONTINUED

LEARNING TO BOWL

Lesson 1: Gripping the Ball

The bowling ball is gripped with 3 fingers, the middle finger, the index finger and the thumb, which fit into the 3 special holes provided.

Hold hand with these three fingers pointing downward, fold the others back, approach ball rack, and slip fingers into holes in bowling ball.

Grasp bowling ball firmly and lift. You are now ready for the next important step in learning to bowl: The Approach. Carry ball... OOOPS!

One important thing we forgot to tell you about gripping the ball... Be sure your fingers aren't greasy ...and that holes aren't too big!

Lesson 2: The Approach

The important thing in the approach is to have perfect form. Start with feet together. Now, take a 14 inch step with your left foot (1), followed quickly by your right foot, stepping about twice that distance (2). Slow up on the next left, which is another 14 inch step (3). Then cross over with your right foot, and slide on it. You'll find this to be rather awkward for bowling but on a dance floor, with the right music, it's a terrific Mambo!

MAGIC-EYE CAMERA SEQUENCE CATCHES PERFECT BOWLING ALLEY FORM

In bowling, form is everything. Perfect bowling-alley form is captured by the magic-eye camera in this special series of...of...OVA-VA-VOOM! Aw, c'mon fellows! Hey Fellows! Pay attention! That's not the perfect bowling alley form we're talking about. Let's try it again, Hey fellows?

Now, the magic-eye camera catches the...Oh! just one other thing we forgot to tell you about gripping the ball...make sure the holes are big enough!

A GLOSSARY OF FAMILIAR BOWLING TERMS...

SPLIT

What happens when you go bowling in tight pants.

FOUL LINE

What you'll hear when you forget the pinboy's tip.

ALLEY

Where you'll sleep when you get home from bowling at 3 AM!

A SIMPLE OUTLINE OF HOW TO SCORE IN BOWLING...

Scoring is a fascinating and enjoyable part of the game of bowling. If you know how to score, you are indeed fortunate, mainly because scoring gives you a chance to sit down. Here, then, is a brief simple outline of how to keep score. To make it even simpler, we have supplied a typical score (above) which you can follow while learning. Ready? Then here goes...

A game of bowling consists of ten innings, or frames. There are ten pins set up for each frame, and you have two balls, or chances to knock as many of them down as you can. If you knock down, say, seven pins with your two balls in the first frame, you put a seven in the first frame's big box. No, the little box is not for the score the midgets bowling in the next alley make, the little box is in case you make a spare or a strike. If you knock down all ten pins with your two balls, that is a spare. If you knock down all ten pins with your first ball, that is a strike. If you make a spare, you don't put anything down in the big box, you put a spare sign in the little box. This gives you ten pins plus the amount of pins you knock down with your next ball. If you get a strike, you put a strike sign in the little box, and this gives you ten pins plus the amount of pins you knock down with your next two balls. Thus, if you get a spare in the first frame, and you knock down eight pins with the first ball in the second frame, you can see that you get eighteen in the first frame. If you get a strike in the first frame and knock down nine pins with both balls in the second frame, you can see that you get nineteen in the first frame and nine more in the second frame, for a total of twenty-eight.

However, if you get ten pins with both balls in the second frame, you can see that this gives you twenty points in the first frame and a spare sign in the second frame, which means that in the second frame, you'll add ten points to the twenty in the first frame plus the amount of pins you knock down with the first ball in the third frame. Now, if you get a strike with the first ball in the second frame, and you already had a strike in the first frame, then you can't put anything down in the first frame because, as you can see, you still have another ball coming which won't be rolled till the third frame. Thus, the pins you knock down with that first ball in the third frame will be added to the ten pins you knocked down with the strike ball in the second frame, and all that will be added to the ten pins you knocked down with the strike ball in the first frame to give you your first frame's score. Then, the pins you knock down with the second ball you roll in the third frame will be added to the pins you knocked down with the first ball in the third frame, and that will be added to the ten pins you knocked down with the strike ball in the second frame which will be added to the score in the first frame to give you the score in the second frame. Now, if you happen to get a strike with the first ball you roll in the third frame, then you still owe one more ball to the second frame which won't be rolled till the fourth frame, and which will be the first of the two you owe to the third frame, and . . .

Well, as you can see, when it comes to scoring, here is one place where you can get rid of plenty pent-up hostility.

FAMOUS RECORD HOLDERS IN BOWLING

JOHN L. LEWIS

Seventeen Strikes in a Row

TOMMY MANVILLE

Eleven Splits in a Row

OSGOOD Z'BEARD

Nineteen Pinboys in a Row

** We may be wrong but all women seem shorter when they take off their shoes.

WESTERN DEPT.

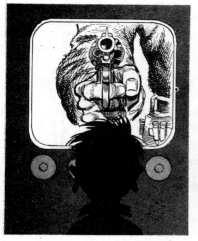   

AND NOW MAD PRESENTS ITS OWN VERSION OF THE REALISTIC WESTERN TV PROGRAM THAT BEGINS WITH AN UNUSUALLY REALISTIC WESTERN FLAVOR.

MAINLY, THIS PROGRAM BEGINS BY FIRST KILLING OFF THE TV AUDIENCE

PICTURES BY JACK DAVIS

GUNSMOKED

"This here is Boot Hill. Many men are buried here. Some 'cause they were good, some 'cause they were bad. But all, 'cause they were dead, by George!"

"My name's Madd Dillinger. I'm DeSoto City's U.S. Marshal. I'm responsible for puttin' most of these men here in Boot Hill. Yuh see, I'm also DeSoto City's grave-digger."

"Every week, I come up here t' Boot Hill, take off m' hat, look down, an' remember a story from the old days in DeSoto City. I look down an' I remember the story 'cause I got the script hid right here in the sweatband!"

GUNSMOKED CONTINUED

STORY MIGHT START WITH A SHOOTIN' IN LAST STRAW SALOON WHILE MARSHAL IS OUT OF TOWN

... OR STORY MIGHT START WITH SHOOTIN' IN LIVERY STABLE WHILE MARSHAL IS OUT OF TOWN

IN ANY CASE, YOU CAN BET STORY WILL START WHILE MARSHAL M. DILLINGER IS OUT OF TOWN

** Guys who stagger into doorways to take a slug of Vitalis are even money to become alcoholics.

GUNSMOKED CHARACTERS TYPIFY HIGH-TYPE CITIZENS WHO PIONEERED WEST

CLIMAX OF GUNSMOKED STORY COMES WHEN TOLERANT MARSHAL FACES KILLER

Story might end with Marshal leavin' the killer in custody of a special deputy...

...or story might end with Marshal leavin' killer in custody of horse trough...

In any case, you can bet story will end with Marshal Dillinger leavin' town...

EACH WEEK, THERE IS A BIG TV. SHOW COMES ON THE AIR WHICH OPENS LIKE THIS:

AND EACH WEEK, WHEN THIS SHOW COMES ON THE AIR, IT OPENS WORLDS LIKE THIS:

A broken promise of things to come.

True tales made up from the legendary past.

The wonderland of Nature's own film.

The happiest world of them all—for kids.

BUT MAINLY, EACH WEEK WHEN THIS SHOW COMES ON THE AIR, IT REALLY OPENS THIS:

The Happy Happy Happiest World of them all
—for Walt Dizzy

TV DEPT.   период

AND NOW, HERE IS HOST WALT DIZZY, WHO USUALLY INTRODUCES DIZZYLAND

This scrap-book contains many fond memories for me. For example, it contains scenes from my first animated cartoon... er...now...what *was* that title?

This scrap-book also contains scenes from my first feature-length animated movie, "Snow...something..." The title slips my mind at the moment...

OOOPS!

Heh, Heh! *Wrong scrap-book!* This scrap-book contains the first dollar I ever made, U.S. silver certificate, series of 1920, Serial No. A-5017234-J!

Making animated cartoons is an exacting art. It takes roughly 50,000 separate cells or drawings to make one cartoon. I keep a set of 50,000 cells in each of these drawers...

For example, this drawer contains the 50,000 cells I made for my first Darnold Duck cartoon back in nineteen thirty...

OOOPS!

Heh, Heh! *Wrong drawer!* This drawer contains the 50,000 bills my first Darnold Duck cartoon made for me!

In this cabinet are the intricate models I made for my feature movie "20,000 Grand...er... LEAGUES under the..." OOOPS! *Wrong cabinet!*

Pardon me a moment folks, while I just get a broom out of this broom closet and sweep up a bit... *OOOPS! WRONG CLOSET!*

Quick! Let's switch to Jimmy Dood in the Music Room!—Say, that's not Jimmy Dood! OOOPS! *WRONG ROOM!*

** The horses at the Trotters would run a lot faster if they didn't have to pull those wagons.

DIZZYLAND CONTINUED

ADVENTURESLAND..the Wonder plac

REAL-LIVE ADVENTURES CAMERAMAN WAITS YEAR FOR SHOT OF RARE BIRD

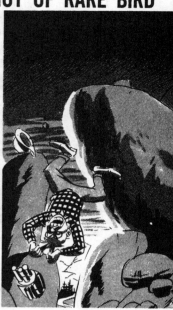

OZGOOD ZEISS, Dizzyland Real-Live Adventures ace cameraman perches on mountain ledge, awaits rare appearance of the never-before-photographed Ring-Necked Fuzzwort.

CAMERA READY, Ozgood waits... and waits. Summer wanes, Autumn leaves begin to fall, and Winter snows begin, but still no Fuzzwort. Determined Ozgood clings to perch.

SPRING THAW comes, and one year passes. Finally, after twenty month vigil, Fuzzwort makes appearance. Jubilant Ozgood takes history making chance-of-a-lifetime shot...

THEN, as Fuzzwort disappears again, Ozgood flings himself screaming from ledge, realizing that chance-of-a-lifetime shot is ruined. Dated film in camera had expired...

TOMORROWSLAND..a Broken Promis

FANTASTIC LOOK INTO FUTURE EXAMINES PROBLEMS OF MAN IN OUTER SPACE

TOMORROWSLAND FEATURE graphically depicts most vital problem yet to be solved before man can venture forth into outer space: the vital problem of zero-gravity, or state of total weightlessness where things float about in a free-fall.

DIZZYLAND ARTISTS work overtime in experimental vacuum-sealed studio, to create realistic animated sequences showing how free-fall problem is solved, like using webbed beds, plastic drinking bags, rubber-lined walls, and mainly plenty glue.

DIZZYLAND ARTISTS were able to create convincing, realistic animated sequences showing how problem is solved after experiencing free-fall in person. Thoughtful management forced entire staff to make mass leap from 10th floor studio window.

我渴的很

Nature's own Film
REAL-LIVE ADVENTURES PHOTOGRAPHER POSES AS BUFFALO TO GET CLOSE-UPS

SIGISMUND (Ciggy) SPONK, Dizzyland Real-Live Adventures trump cameraman employs clever (but uncomfortable) trick of draping himself with moth-eaten buffalo skin in ruse to sneak up through sagebrush to get breath-taking close up of herd.

CLEVER RUSE succeeds. Placidly grazing buffalo take no notice as disguised (and uncomfortable) Sigismund creeps into midst of herd and, setting up his hand-held combat-type 16 mm camera, begins shooting history-making close-up footage..

CLEVER TRICK backfires as magnificent herd bull, snorting and pawing ground, takes sudden fancy to charming (but uncomfortable) newcomer, decides to make Sigismund his happy bride. Plenty history-making close-up footage was lost in chase!

Things to Come
VIVID STORY TRACES ROCKET DEVELOPMENT FROM NOVEL TOY TO PRESENT DAY

INFORMATIVE Tomorrowsland feature depicts history of rockets starting with invention as novel toy by Ancient Chinese and shows honorable inventors having much honorable fun...

FEATURE TRACES development from novel toy to have honorable fun with to first practical use with interesting attempt to send the mail via rockets in early nineteen-twenties.

FEATURE GOES ON to show how novel toy to have honorable fun with was developed by Germans during World War II into effective weapon of dishonorable 'fun,' the dreaded V-2.

FEATURE COMES up to date by showing scientists at White Sands making countless experimental launchings of latest rocket types. By George...! We're back having honorable fun...

** We sincerely believe Ernest Hemingway to be a greater writer than Mickey Spillane.

DIZZYLAND CONTINUED

FRONTREARLAND ...True Tales Made u

EXPLOITS OF FORMERLY UNHERALDED PIONEER HEROES TEACH T

Competition

Resourcefulness

TRADITIONAL AMERICAN SPIRIT of competition is conveyed during exciting keelboat race as raggle-taggle crews of Davy Crawcutt and Mike Finque eagerly pole their way down Mississippi River.

DESPERATE ATTEMPTS of Mike Finque and Davy Crawcutt to win keelboat race clearly illustrates for youth of this generation importance of relying upon honest American skill and ingenuity.

FANTASTICLAND ...the Happiest World

- The happiest world of them all?!?
- What's so happy about it?
- Actually we're *miserable!*
- Don't get the idea because we're drawn smiling, we're happy!
- Used to be, we were big-shots around the Dizzy studios!
- Used to be, we were the whole darn show!
- Some thanks we get...a being responsible for all of Dizzy's success!

om the Legendary Past
Y'S YOUTH RESPECT FOR TIME-HONORED AMERICAN TRADITIONS

Teamwork | Sportsmanship | Leadership

TYPICAL AMERICAN tradition of teamwork is depicted as Mike and Davy cooperate in sinking fleet of attacking Indian canoes.

GOOD OLD AMERICAN sportsmanship tradition is shown by Davy Crawcutt when he fails to shoot ale cup off Mike's head.

FINE AMERICAN attribute of leadership is shown when Davy enters Congress and declares he can lick any man in the House!

hem All.

...in favor of movies with REAL LIVE ANIMALS... and REAL LIVE PEOPLE!

Sometimes he even makes us *act* in them!

Walt may tell you he's doing it mainly to try out new things...

Walt may tell you he's doing it mainly for kicks!

The truth is...

...he's doing it mainly for *money!*

** Somehow sandhogs never seem to get a suntan.

PSYCHOLOGY DEPT.

**Two heads are better than one
—Patience and Prudence

You know how every once in a while you stop suddenly in the middle of flapping the lower lip, and you wonder if maybe you're crazy? Well, you don't have to wonder any more. Now you can be sure. Because, today, high-priced psychiatrists have fool-proof tests which can prove you're a fool. Like, f'rinstance, there's the famous Rorschach Test, where you look at these interesting ink blots and tell the psychiatrist what they look like to you . . . and then he tells what you look like to him. The only trouble with that test is . . . it costs about forty or fifty dollars. Which brings us to the purpose of this next article:

Now, as a service to those of you who have stopped suddenly in the middle of flapping the lower lip and wondered, MAD saves you money, eliminates the middle-man, and allows you, in the privacy of your own home, to find out once and for all if you're crazy. So don't be chicken. Go ahead. Take . . .

MAD'S INK BLOT TEST

Directions: These ink blots were scientifically designed by a psychiatrist friend of ours who gave up his practice after he suffered a nervous breakdown from listening to his patients' constant complaining. Study each blot for a moment and let it suggest something to you. Then see if it matches the analysis below each blot. Hey . . . no cheating!

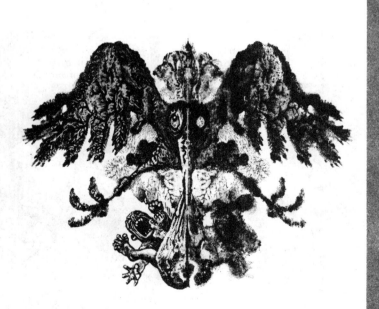

IF this ink blot looks to you like a stork delivering twins, then you are obviously emotionally immature, since any grown-up knows that storks don't bring babies.

IF this ink blot appears to be a bartender loaded with two kegs of whiskey, then watch out. Your subconscious mind indicates that you are a potential alcoholic.

PICTURES BY KELLY FREAS

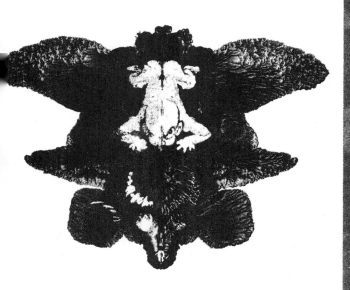

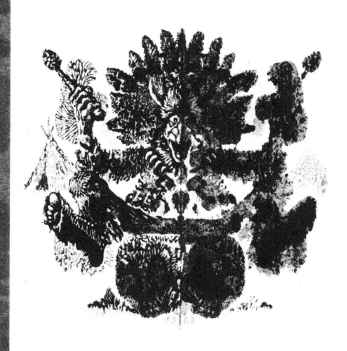

IF this blot resembles a baby on a bear skin rug, then you are emotionally inhibited. Let yourself go, man! A *babe* on a bear skin rug is what you *should* be seeing!

IF this blot suggests an American Indian pounding a war drum, then you obviously have repressed hostilities. You'd like to beat up somebody named Tom . . . *twice*.

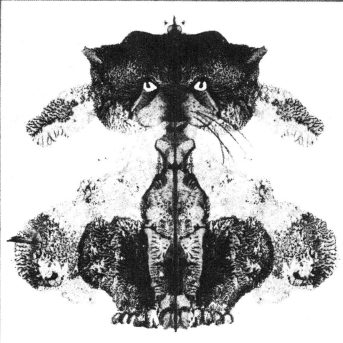

IF this ink blot bears a likeness to two swordsmen engaged in an affair of honor, battling to the death, beware! Your reaction shows you have a duel personality.

IF this blot looks like a squatting cat, you're definitely crazy! Not 'cause you see a squatting cat. You're crazy to spend good money on trash like MAD magazine!

***Don't kill the goose that lays golden eggs*
—Dean Martin

HOLLYWOOD DEPT.
SCENES WE'D LIKE TO SEE

**Wanted ... an idea for a new-type magazine. —Hugh Hefner

The Faithful Dog

SOFT-SELL ADVERTISING DEPT.

It's time for the commercial, gang, so here we go with another example of how Madison Avenue will probably overdo a good thing like the "Harry and Bert Piel" commercials, with this sample story board of a...

FUTURE TV AD

STORY BOARD BY DON MARTIN — CONTINUED ON NEXT PAGE

DATING DEPT.

Since you are obviously a failure in the dating department, (You wouldn't be wasting time reading this trash if you could be going out with girls!) MAD now offers you a rare opportunity to overcome your difficulties with this article which explains...

THE MAD DATING TECHNIQUE

Up to now, you have probably approached the problem of dealing with the fair sex in one of two ways. You've either been the "shy" type, and you've failed miserably, or you've been the "aggressive" type, and you've failed miserably. Now, MAD shows you how to be the "Mad" type, and fail miserably. All kidding aside though, let's go through a typical date, and see how these three types would handle the very same situations. When you've finished, it will be obvious to you that you've made many bad mistakes in your time, including starting this article in the first place.

**Wanted... travelling companion. —John Foster Dulles

THE SHY TYPE
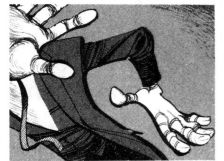

THE AGGRESSIVE TYPE

THE MAD TYPE

ASKING FOR THE DATE

THE SHY TYPE hasn't enough nerve to ask for date, writes note instead, pays kid to deliver it. Unfortunately, girl usually accepts, goes out with the kid.

THE AGRESSIVE TYPE has plenty of nerve, asks girl for date right out. Unfortunately the girl also has plenty of nerve and she usually refuses outright.

THE MAD TYPE doesn't bother to ask, shows up at the girl's house with flowers, asks if she's ready. She hasn't enough nerve to admit she forgot date.

SECURING TRANSPORTATION

THE SHY TYPE hasn't the nerve to ask for his old man's car, so he rents one.

THE AGGRESSIVE TYPE doesn't even ask for his old man's car, he just steals it.

THE MAD TYPE not only borrows old man's car, he also borrows the old man.

IMPRESSING THE GIRL'S FATHER

CHALLENGED BY DATE'S FATHER to Indian wrestle, the shy type purposely loses match, impresses father as a clod.

CHALLENGED BY DATE'S FATHER to Indian wrestle, the aggressive type throws father, impresses him as a clod.

CHALLENGED BY DATE'S FATHER to Indian wrestle, the MAD type throws mother, impresses father as great guy.

*****Wanted . . . a girl I can love for herself alone.
—Porfirio Rubirosa*

PLANNING WHERE TO GO

THE SHY TYPE, in search of place offering possibilities of little conversation, takes his date to neighborhood movie.

THE AGGRESSIVE TYPE, in search of place offering possibilities of little $ investment, takes his date to same movie.

THE MAD TYPE in search of place offering possibilities of a little necking, takes his date to balcony of the same movie.

IMPRESSING THE GIRL FINANCIALLY

THE SHY TYPE impresses his date by inadvertently leaving a big tip. He's too chicken to ask the waiter for change.

THE AGGRESSIVE TYPE impresses his date by impulsively leaving big tip. He eats candy-bar lunches all that week.

THE MAD TYPE impresses his date by deliberately leaving a big tip. He cleverly swipes it all back as he leaves table.

**Wanted . . . a girl who will love me for myself alone.
—Tommy Manville

LOOKING FOR A LITTLE PRIVACY

THE SHY TYPE stops car, pulls old routine about being out of gas. Date gets mad, so he ends up walking down dark lonely road to distant service station.

THE AGGRESSIVE TYPE stops car, pulls 'out-of-gas' routine. Date gets mad, he gets mad, so she ends up walking down lonely dark road to a distant bus stop.

THE MAD TYPE doesn't resort to any corny routines. He crashes the car into a tree, and they *both* end up walking down that dark lonely road. Hoo-hah!

KISSING THE GIRL GOODNIGHT

THE SHY TYPE hasn't the nerve to kiss his date goodnight, puckers several times, and finally ends up whistling.

THE AGGRESSIVE TYPE grabs his date forcefully, kisses her several times, and finally ends up nursing a black eye...

THE MAD TYPE doesn't try, turns to go, falls down, bumps mouth, finally ends up with date kissing his booboo...

**Wanted... a new T.V. show for Phil Silvers.
—The U.S. Army

TOM LEHRER DEPT.

TOM LEHRER SINGS

MR. TOM LEHRER

And now, MAD presents the words and music to one of Tom Lehrer's inimitable songs, in spite of widespread popular demand for its suppression, primarily for the benefit of a small but diminishing group of admirers of his dubious talents . . . talents which have been on display for several years at functions, orgies, and divers festive occasions around Harvard University where he was in attendance until June, 1953, as an undergraduate, graduate student, and teacher of mathematics. A few television and night club appearances have also been part of his infamous career. Some of his songs, which have been revolting local audiences for years, are now available in his song book* and on his LP record**, and it is no wonder that a great deal of public apathy has been stirred up by the prospect. For those who are unfamiliar with the details of his sordid life, brought so vividly to the screen in *Quo Vadis,* we offer a brief biographical note:

Tom Lehrer, longtime exponent of the *dèrriere-garde* in American music, is an entirely mythical figure, a figment of his parents' warped imagination. He was raised by a yak, by whom he was always treated as one of the family, and ever since he was old enough to eat with the grownups, he has been merely the front for a vast international syndicate of ne'er-do-wells. But enough of Lehrer the artist. What of Lehrer, the *bon vivant,* man about town, and idol of three continents (and Madagascar, where half a million gibbering natives think he is God)? At last report, he had been uprooted from his home in Cambridge, Mass., where he'd earned a precarious living peddling dope to the local school children and rolling an occasional drunk, and summoned into the service of his country, namely entertaining the brass. It will be some time before Mr. Lehrer can return to his shrunken head collection, his Nobel Prizes, and his memories.

This particular song is reprinted from his song book. As Al Capp writes in its introduction: *"The advantage of Tom Lehrer's song book over his record album is that you are spared his voice. Not that his is an unpleasant voice. It is an offended voice. And this is not surprising, for his is an offended spirit. He is offended by ideas that we have accepted unquestioningly all our lives, perhaps with secret misgivings, but without protest. With his songs, Tom Lehrer protests. And that is not surprising either, because, since he was a student and a teacher at Harvard when these songs were written, he hadn't much else to do."*

This song is a 20th Century cowboy ballad about the wonders of the present day Wild West, as described by the few news stories that penetrate to the East.

**Wanted . . . building site in a low-rent district. —Robert Hall

THE WILD WEST IS WHERE I WANT TO BE

A--long the trail you'll find me lopin',
Where the spaces are wide open,
In the land of the old A.E.C. (Ya-hoo)

Where the scenery's attractive
And the air is radioactive,
Oh the Wild West is where I want to be!

'Mid the sagebrush and the cactus
I'll watch the fellers practice
Droppin' bombs through the clean desert breeze. (Ya-hoo!)

I'll have on my sombrero
And of course I'll wear a pair o'
Levis over my lead B.V.D.'s.

PICTURES BY GEORGE WOODBRIDGE

I will leave the city's rush,
Leave the fancy and the plush,
Leave the snow and leave the slush,
And the crowds.

I will seek the desert's hush,
Where the scenery is lush,
How I long to see the mush--
room clouds.

'Mid the yuccas and the thistles
I'll watch the guided missiles,
While the old F.B.I. watches me. (Ya-Hoo!)

Yes, I'll soon make my appearance,
(Soon as I can get my clearance)
'Cause the Wild West is where I want to be.

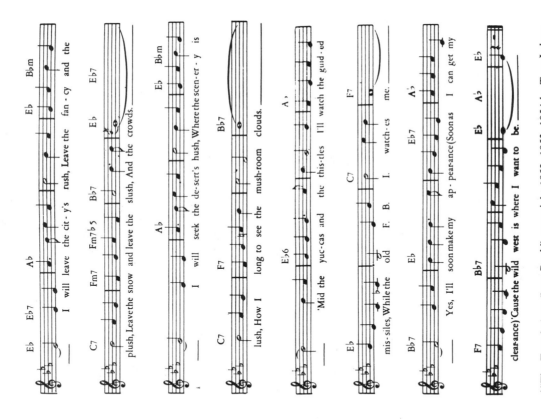
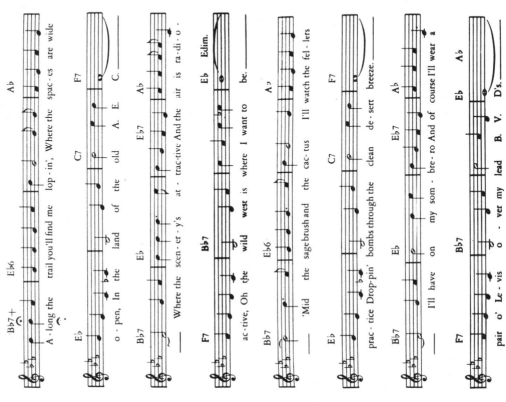

WILD LIFE DEPT.

This next article by MAD's maddest artist, Don Martin, was drawn to illustrate a problem he's been having lately... a problem which he calls...

THE UNFORTUNATE PART OF FEEDING PIGEONS HOMEMADE POPCORN

ART AND CONTINUITY BY DON MARTIN

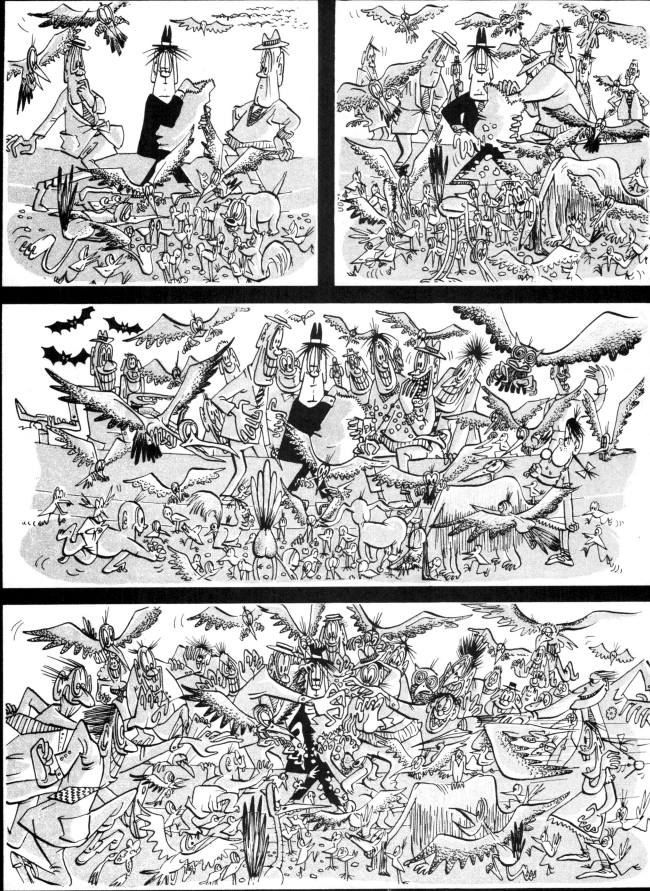

CONTINUED ON NEXT PAGE

We'd like to be Norman Vincent Peale's psychiatrist.

SECTION 8 DEPT.

**We'd like to be an elevator man in a one-story building.

The following article by Frank Jacobs immediately convinced us that he is a "MAD" writer. We were convinced when this article was brought to us by Mr. Jacob's literary agent, who curiously wore a white coat. Here, then, is Frank's frank confession on...

WHY I LEFT THE ARMY AND BECAME A CIVILIAN

IN THE ARMY
...if I didn't get out of the sack at 6 A.M., my sergeant would blow his top!

AS A CIVILIAN
...I enjoy the luxury of sleeping as long as I want and getting up when I feel like it.

PICTURES BY GEORGE WOODBRIDGE

IN THE ARMY
...I had to put on my uniform, and stand freezing outside the barracks, waiting for the Captain.

AS A CIVILIAN
...I dress as I please, and stand freezing at the railroad station, waiting for the 8:36.

CONTINUED ON NEXT PAGE

IN THE ARMY

. . . I had to rub elbows with my entire platoon at breakfast, and had to eat what everyone else ate.

AS A CIVILIAN

. . . I breakfast at a friendly drugstore near my office, and I eat whatever I feel like eating.

IN THE ARMY

. . . if I were late for duty, I'd get chewed out by the Captain.

AS A CIVILIAN

. . . I get to the office when I please. No one checks on me.

IN THE ORDERLY ROOM

. . . I had to lick the Colonel's boots when he came to inspect.

IN THE AD AGENCY

. . . I bow to no one. The client comes to me with humble requests.

AS A P.F.C.
... I always had the feeling that the other P.F.C.s were trying to beat me out of my Corporal's promotion.

IN THE ARMY
... whenever I'd get an official memo, I'd always be scared it was a transfer to some distant outpost ...

AS AN ACCOUNT EXECUTIVE
... I feel secure in my job. No one is after it. I know I'll be moved up fairly, on my own merit.

IN THE AD AGENCY
... whenever I get my pay envelope, I open it with confidence, knowing that all is well ...

*We'd like to be Yul Brynner's barber.

ARMY LIFE DROVE ME NUTS
... so I left the service the first chance I got and became a civilian.

IN CIVILIAN LIFE
... my experience is in demand. I know I can always get a job with another firm.

OUT OF LEFT FIELD DEPT.

WE HERE AT MAD ARE ALL FOR FIGHTING JUVENILE DELINQUENCY. BUT WE ARE FOR FIGHTING THIS PROBLEM INTELLIGENTLY AND SCIENTIFICALLY. WE JUST CAN'T TAKE SERIOUSLY THOSE PSEUDO-EXPERTS WHO COME FORWARD FROM TIME TO TIME WITH ARTICLES PROCLAIMING CURE-ALLS FOR THIS VAST AND COMPLICATED PROBLEM. ARTICLES LIKE THIS:

BASEBALL IS RUINING OUR

THE BATTER'S function consists of swinging a lethal weapon, a club, with all of his brute strength, at a defenseless ball, with the sole purpose of smashing it as far as he can. From this act, our impressionable children learn, wrongly, that *the stronger you are, the greater will be your reward.*

PICTURES BY WALLACE WOOD

THE BUNT is another form of batting the ball. The player, who is expected to swing hard at the ball, suddenly switches his stance in order to tap a pitch lightly down in front of the plate, catching his opponent off-guard. Here, our young people learn that *sneaky tactics are also rewarded . . .*

Society is like a garden, and our children are like flowers that bud, grow, and bloom there. Unfortunately, in today's garden, many of our flowers are going bad. The fact is, they're turning into stinkweeds! When *one* weak flower goes bad in a garden, it is nothing to worry about. But when *many* flowers begin going bad in a garden, that *is* something to worry about. Pretty soon the whole place will be one awful mess!

Today, juvenile delinquency plagues society. Thousands of flowers are going bad in our garden. It's time we exposed the cause. And it is not Japanese Beetles!

The cause can be found right smack in the middle of our garden . . . on the grass . . . where they play "Baseball"!

For many years, I worked closely with "juvenile delinquents". Then my hair turned gray, and they kicked me out of their gang. But while I was with them, I studied them. I questioned them, probed their minds, uncovered their ids, examined their egos, and rifled their pockets. And in every single case I examined, I repeatedly came up with the same shocking fact: *At one time or another, every one of those poor misguided children had been exposed to the game of "Baseball"!* They had either *played* it themselves, or *watched* it being played . . . not to mention the countless other indirect exposures such as "Baseball Magazines", "Baseball Record Books", and the worst offender of all, "Baseball Bubble-Gum Cards".

Yes, the game of "Baseball" is souring the soil of society's garden, rotting our flowering youth.

Let me analyze this "game" for you. Let me expose the psychological undertones present in this so-called "sport".

A SHOESTRING CATCH describes the action of a player who runs in and retrieves an otherwise safely-hit ball before it touches the ground, literally catching it at his shoes. Such a feat usually earns a burst of applause, teaching that *to deprive another of what is rightfully his is a laudable act.*

Dr. Frederick Werthless, shown above, gathering material for this article from the "Dodger Yearbook", interviewed hundreds of teen-age delinquents as they left Children's Courts all over the U.S. "The evidence was overwhelming!" states Dr. Werthless. "Almost every delinquent child brought into court had a past record of either playing or watching baseball!"

CHILDREN

by FREDERICK WERTHLESS, M.D.

And I can do this! After all, I'm a *Psychiatrist!*

The very essence of "Baseball" is "hostile aggression"! Take, for example, the act of "Batting". The function of the "batter" is to swing a lethal weapon, a club, with all his brute strength, at a defenseless ball, with the sole purpose of smashing it as hard and as far as he can. The harder and further he smashes it, the greater his reward!

What kind of healthy example is this for our youth?

With his act of brute force successfully completed, the "batter" seeks out safety by running to first base. *Runs,* mind you, like a thief in the night.

Is he so plagued with guilt that he cannot walk?

The opposition, a team of nine equally "hostile" and "aggressive" men, whose purpose is to deprive the "batter" of his desire to reach safety, pounce upon the "violence-inflicted" ball, and attempt to relay it to the protector of a base before the "batter" can arrive.

An arbiter, dressed in a uniform subtly suggestive of a policeman, judges the play and makes his decision. Consequently, only one of the protagonists can be pleased. The other must rebel!

He defies authority as our children watch!

And so it goes through the course of the game . . . one disgraceful exhibition after another . . . deplorable examples for our impressionable youth.

Study the pictures on these pages, and the documented case-histories on the following page . . . and see if you don't conclude that BASEBALL IS RUINING OUR CHILDREN . . . that the "game" should be banned, the players committed to institutions and the stadiums turned into parking lots!

BREAKING UP THE DOUBLE PLAY, a despicable practice, consists of a runner's sliding into a base with spikes high. The base player, in avoiding these lethal blades, cannot get his throw away, and is lucky to get away himself. Here, our younger generation learns *the advantages of dirty tactics . . .*

ARGUING WITH AN UMPIRE is the usual practice in baseball. If a player does not happen to agree with a decision, he enters into heated disagreement with the arbiter, to the point of name-calling and nose-thumbing. From this display, children learn that *rebellion against authority is acceptable.*

THE PITCHER uses many deliveries calculated to cause the batter to miss. These consist of assorted fast balls which curve, drop and even slide. Then, he uses a complete change of pace, the so-called "let-up" pitch, confusing the batter, and implanting in young minds *the evil seeds of deception.*

DOCUMENTED CASE-HISTORIES PROVE THAT NORMAL DESIRES TO IMITATE BASEBALL HEROES TURN ORDINARY CHILDREN INTO JUVENILE DELINQUENTS

CASE No. 36

Irving Smedley, age 11, was brought into Children's Court on a charge of having slammed a playmate on the head with a stick. Irving could not logically explain why he did it.

A search of Irving's pockets uncovered the above "Bubble-Gum Card" showing Ted Williams slamming a baseball with a bat. Obviously this is where young Smedley got the idea.

CASE No. 47

Sidney Finster, age 9, was arrested by authorities as the culprit responsible for a series of crimes in which stray animals were found with their natural coats of fur missing.

Subsequent investigation, which included a search of Sidney's room, uncovered a sports magazine with the above testimonial. Obviously, Sidney attempted to emulate his hero.

CASE No. 64

Melvin Cowznofski, age 12, was apprehended while attempting to steal valuable sculpture from local art museum. He could offer no explanation for taking the Work of Art . . .

Melvin's belongings included a copy of the Dodger Yearbook, containing the above picture of Pee Wee Reese attempting to steal a base. Obviously, Melvin had tried to outdo him.

Next issue, Dr. Werthless continues with the second installment: "The Little League, Hotbed of Juvenile Crime."

HOLLYWOOD DEPT.

Scenes We'd Like to See

Driving The Golden Spike

ART—GEORGE WOODBRIDGE   STORY BY EUGENE ST. JEAN

SEEING IS BELIEVING DEPT.

You've heard about this "Picture-Phone"... the coming telephone system where you not only hear, but see the person you're talking to? Well, we at MAD are worried about a big problem its use is sure to create. And we're not talking about the problem: How you gonna answer the "Picture-Phone" when it rings while you're taking a bath? This is no problem for us, since we don't take baths. What we're worried about is the problem: How you gonna tell them little white lies, when the people you're trying to fool can see for themselves you're a faker? The solution, as we see it, is: Some smart operators... Us, for example!... should bring out a kit specifically designed for fooling people on "Picture-Phone". You would merely tell them little white lies while standing before old window shades cleverly converted into:

MAD'S PICTURE-PHONE BACKDROPS

PICTURES BY GEORGE WOODBRIDGE

*The trouble with people is their trouble with people.

FOOL YOUR WIFE...

Sorry, Dear! I'm stuck here at the office again tonight! Don't bother to wait up...

FOOL YOUR BOSS...

Can't make it in, today, J. B.! Got a bad cold! The doc says I should stay right here in bed...

** A woman may not mind your lying about the size of your yacht, but don't expect her to do the rowing.

ERNIE KOVACS DEPT. PART I

Strangely Believe It!

PICTURES BY WALLACE WOOD

TOULOUSE LA FEINSTEIN

A Grocery Clerk From ALTOONA, PENNSYLVANIA, Although He Had Never Held A Brush In His Hand, **PAINTED A PICTURE THAT SOLD FOR $137,000!**

TOULOUSE HAD MISTAKENLY PAINTED IT ON THE BACK OF AN ORIGINAL DA VINCI

IT IS POSSIBLE TO GET DRUNK ON CANTALOUPE!

A CALIFORNIA-GROWN CANTALOUPE, IF SUFFICIENTLY SUN-RIPENED, SPRINKLED LIBERALLY WITH POWDERED SUGAR, AND WARMED IN A 200° OVEN, CAN CAUSE THE EATER TO BECOME STAGGERING DRUNK... When Washed Down With A Fifth Of Bourbon.

CENTIPEDES CAN BE TRAINED TO DIVE!

However, no Centipede has ever performed this Athletic Feat in Public... As Centipedes Have No Hipbones, And Their Swimming Trunks Keep Falling Down.

LEONARD RAPPAPORT HAS NOT SHAVED IN 52 YEARS! THAT'S BECAUSE LEONARD RAPPAPORT IS A WOMAN.

MRS. IRMA T. GRIBNEY, A Housewife From Brokenhorn, Texas, IS THE MOTHER OF 8 CHILDREN, EACH BORN ON A DIFFERENT DAY OF THE WEEK!

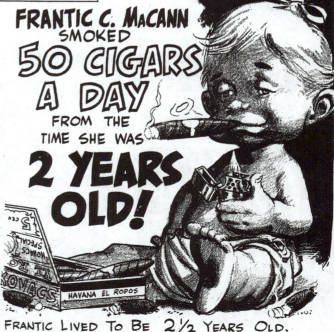

FRANTIC C. MACANN SMOKED **50 CIGARS A DAY** FROM THE TIME SHE WAS **2 YEARS OLD!**

FRANTIC LIVED TO BE 2½ YEARS OLD.

DAVY JONES' LOCKER DEPT.

Here's a refreshing new angle on bathing and beach sports as practised by MAD's maddest artist, Don Martin, in this account which he calls...

THE SEASIDE INCIDENT

CONTINUED ON NEXT PAGE

"I'm Forever Blowing Bubbles" —Lawrence Welk

ART AND CONTINUITY BY DON MARTIN

SOUND THINKING DEPT.

If you own a Hi-Fi set, you're a lucky individual. If it works, you're even luckier. Because a Hi-Fi set can turn your living room into a veritable Carnegie Hall. It's even better than the real Carnegie Hall because you're never bothered by late-comers, coughers, program-rustlers, and that $4.80 admission charge. What you are bothered by is hum, distortion, surface noise, and that screaming neighbor. In any case, it looks like Hi-Fi is here to stay, and who are we to fight a trend. So, neighbor, get out your ear-plugs, because in this article

MAD GOES HiFi

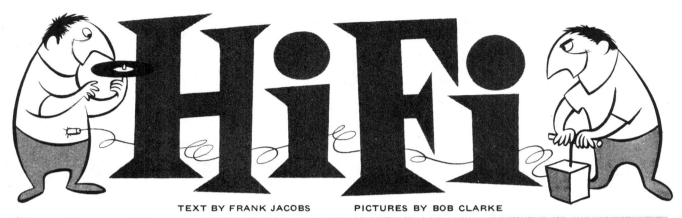

TEXT BY FRANK JACOBS PICTURES BY BOB CLARKE

**SID CAESAR will return a Lawrence Welk album

A GLOSSARY OF HI-FI TERMS
(So you'll know what we're talking about. We don't!)

HIGH FIDELITY—Full, faithful reproduction of recorded sound.
LOW FIDELITY—Porfirio Rubirosa
LOUDSPEAKER—Person who talks while Hi-Fi set is on.
WOOFER—Dog who talks while Hi-Fi set is on.
TWEETER—A shade stronger than tweet.
TUNER—A salt water fish.
BASS—See TUNER
TREBLE—"Elbert" spelled backwards, honoring Elbert J. Stylus, only man to be trapped on a revolving 78 rpm turntable for 24 hours and live.
AMPLIFIER—What you make to burn an ampli.
OHM—Where Hi-Fi fan sets up equipment.
PICKUP—Someone to listen to Hi-Fi records with.
WOW—Listening to Hi-Fi records with loose pickup.
FLUTTER—Reaction during Wow.
RESISTOR—What you should do with loose pickup.
AM—Midnight to Noon.
FM—Initials of Felix Mulvaney, first man to faithfully record the belch of an owl.
DIAMOND NEEDLE—What Hi-Fi guy gets from impatient, marriage-minded girlfriend.
PITCH—What you get from Hi-Fi salesman.
TUBES—They run between New Jersey and New York.
DISTORTION—Happens when you leave Hi-Fi records on radiator.

EAR-CONDITIONING IS ESSENTIAL FOR ENJOYING HIGH FIDELITY SOUNDS

Good Hi-Fi equipment is capable of reproducing sounds between 20 and 40,000 cycles. Unfortunately, the human ear is only capable of hearing sounds to about 15,000 cycles. However, dogs can hear sounds between 15,000 and 40,000 cycles! Pictures below taken over several months show Hi-Fi fan becoming conditioned to Hi-Fi sounds...

HOW TO ASSEMBLE
THE OLD EXPENSIVE WAY

STEP 1: YOUR AMPLIFIER...

Rush out and buy shock-proof, water-proof, anti-magnetic, self-winding, sanforized, cork-tipped, micronite-filtered, "Howling Banshee" 20 Watt Basic Amplifier. Cost: $250.00

STEP 2: YOUR TURNTABLE...

Next, purchase ever-floating, sand-packed, velvet spring, non-neurotic, pre-tranquilized, "Whirling Dervish" X-95, 7-Speed, 4-Shift, 250 Horsepower Turntable. Cost: $125.00

STEP 3: YOUR TUNER...

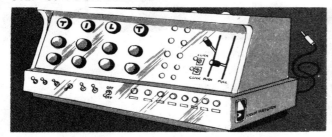

Then order 15-tube, 12-dial, 10-button, 7-switch, 4-light, push-pull, click-click, cross-country, high-strung, over-priced, laminated, "*Caramba*" AM-FM Tuner. Cost: $150.00

STEP 4: YOUR LOUDSPEAKER...

Now shop for birch-faced, six-ply, magic-margin, forward-look, "Little Corporal" Speaker. Cost (including Woofer, Tweeter, Screamer, Shrieker, and Ear-Splitter): $450.00

STEP 5: YOUR REWIRING...

Next step is to rewire your house so you can use all that new Hi-Fi equipment. Cost of rewiring house: $1500.00

STEP 6: YOUR HIGH-VOLTAGE LINES...

Now you have to erect new high-voltage lines from power plant to carry current needed for house. Cost: $20,000

STEP 7: YOUR POWER PLANT...

Finally, you have to construct new power plant to produce enough current now needed for house. Cost: $2,000,000

STEP 8: YOUR HEADACHE...

Now you can sit back, listen to Hi-Fi music, and figure out how you're gonna pay for set. Total Cost: $2,022,475

****MILTON BERLE** will return a television set

YOUR HI-FI SET
THE ECONOMICAL MAD WAY

STEP 1: YOUR AMPLIFIER (AND NEEDLE)...

Scour nearby alleys for mongrel dog with one buck tooth. Plug tail into wall-socket. Output will be surprising! And buck tooth will make fine needle! Cost: Nothing!

STEP 2: YOUR TURNTABLE...

Steal old Lazy Susan Serving-Tray from Dining Room, remove dishes, cover by gluing down sister's old felt skirt, and drive a ten-penny-nail in the center. Cost: Nothing.

STEP 3: YOUR TURNTABLE MOTOR...

Connect turntable to "endless belt" with rope. As howling dog scampers over belt, turntable will revolve. Harness dog's tooth to play LP's. Cost of "endless belt": $2.00

STEP 4: YOUR LOUDSPEAKER...

Mother-in-law makes dandy loudspeaker, as you well know. Merely connect her up to the mongrel dog. Between them, you'll get all the high and low sounds. Cost: Nothing!

STEP 5: YOUR CABINET...

Old barrel found in vacant lot serves as fine cabinet for your Hi-Fi set's components. Cost of barrel: Nothing!

STEP 6: YOUR GOOD FORTUNE...

MAD Hi-Fi set is now finished. You've saved money, and also gotten rid of your Mother-in-law. Total Cost: $2.00

DISGUISE HI-FI EQUIPMENT TO BLEND INTO DECOR FOR BETTER RESULTS

This can be done in various ways. One method is to hide your Hi-Fi components inside various pieces of furniture.

Another method is to hide speakers through house. This will captivate your friends and family wherever they are.

Your week-end guest will certainly get a big kick out of listening to Hi-Fi music while trying to take a shower.

Your daughter and her fiance will surely appreciate the sound of romantic Hi-Fi music while necking in the den.

But mainly, disguise your Hi-Fi set's component parts so your neighbors will have a hard time finding them when they come calling on you after they've been awakened by your blasting away at top volume at 2 AM in the morning.

MAD Reviews New Hi-Fi Recordings

Glass and Steel

FAMOUS AUTOMOBILE CRASHES: *Vol. 1. Sounds of the most spectacular automobile crashes of the past 10 years.* Pleasure Time Records, XM-95 MPH, $4.98

THE LATE Heinrich Baffle, who collected the material for this recording, was a High Fidelity perfectionist to the end. At the time of his death, caused by being caught in the middle of a head-on collision on the Lincoln Highway, Baffle was engaged in the preparation of Volume 2 of this fine series.

Of the 24 crashes recorded here, one that especially lends itself to re-hearing is a 9-car bumper-to-bumper mishap taped on the icy Merritt Parkway during a sleet storm. The lows of steel meeting steel provide a startling contrast to the highs of the motorists' screams.

Most spectacular of all the sounds on this record is the band labeled "Flying Fragments". For this one, Baffle stationed himself in the rock-strewn riverbed, 500 feet below notorious "Hairpin Turn" just outside East Gap, Colorado. Nothing is missing here. The high-cycled sounds of shattering glass, the middle-range shock waves of chrome and metal hitting stone, and the unbelievable low-cycled explosion when the fire reaches the gas tank ... are all faithfully recorded in a technically perfect masterpiece.

Here indeed, is a High-Fidelity record designed for many hours of pleasant Hi-Fi listening.

Sounds of Life

HICCUPS, BELCHES, SNEEZES, AND COUGHS. *Edited by Dr. Bascomb Sneed.* Mucus Records, 2—12" disks, #5007-9, $5.98

TOP NOTCH reproduction, for the most part ... although several of the belches suffer from distortion. The record jacket boasts that the sneezes (performed by actual hospital patients in wards) are so lifelike, they laid up six audio engineers with bad colds and virus during the recording sessions.

Something New in Beethoven

BEETHOVEN: *Symphony No. 3 (The Eroica) with Kyle Linseed playing the solo kazoo.* Longhair Records, 5-J-322, $3.98

HEARING BEETHOVEN rendered on the solo kazoo makes us wonder if the composer really didn't have this instrument in mind when he wrote his masterpiece. As performed by Mr Linseed, the symphony reaches new heights in intensity and power, especially during the finale. At that point, Mr. Linseed, who is the only kazoo player in the world with a forked tongue, nearly shatters the speaker with his magnificent crescendo. The disintegration of his wax paper ends the record in a High-Fidelity coup.

Violence in Nature

BATTLE OF THE ANTS: *Sounds of Nature Series, Vol. 3.* Biology Records, MM-53620456794567-J, $5.98

TO MAKE this record, Hamilton Purge lived in an anthill for seven months, waiting for his chance. "Battle of the Ants" is a thrilling, step-by-step narrative in High-Fidelity sound of a bloody war between two ant armies over a lousy marshmallow. Purge's technical genius has managed to capture all of the marvelous sounds of the conflict ... the insects' call to battle, the shouts of hand-to-hand combat, the cries of victory, and Purge's own screams when his right forearm is used as a minefield.

For devotees of wildlife sounds, this record set will make a worthy addition to your Hi-Fi library. Also recommended are the other offerings in the Sounds of Nature Series: *"Mating Calls of the Seven Year Locusts"*, and *"The Birth of a Water Beetle"*.

Eloquent Elbows

SCHNOOK: *Concerto for Kettledrum and Triangle. Mischa Goss, soloist. J. Hmphlrich, conducting.* Kaput Records, C105, $4.98

NO ONE knows very much about Friedrich Schnook (170?-1?), the German composer who died at the age of seven. We do know that what might have been an impressive career was tragically cut short when the young genius accidentally strangled in the strings of his harp. In any case, his concerto for Kettledrum and Triangle, written when Schnook was six, is a minor masterpiece.

Fortunately for all Schnook lovers, there are 16 versions of this concerto now on records. This latest offering is by far the most impressive, and certainly the most complete. Wisely, the performers have not omitted Schnook's famous, but rarely played Elbow Variation in the third movement. This consists of the soloist striking his kettledrums for 15 minutes with his right elbow, and 10 minutes with his left.

This variation will be of particular interest to High Fidelity fans, as the soloist in this performance misses the kettledrum during the 17th minute, and knocks over the podium.

Letters To The MAD HI-FI Editor

IS IT POSSIBLE?

Dear Hi-Fi Editor,

Is it possible for a printed circuit 40-watt amplifier with an output impedence of 8 ohms and a 70db hum below 35 watts to be connected to a 900 to 20,000 cps 15-omh tweeter with 120° horizontal dispersion and a crossover network of 200 cps when my tuner contains a 3-gang variable condenser, a built-in 20KC whistle filter and three assorted microvolts?

Lance La Touche
Dallas, Texas

It might be fun to try.—Ed.

WRONG WAY?

Dear Hi-Fi Editor,

My turntable persists in revolving in the wrong direction. I cannot listen to my favorite music. What should I do?

Belinda Matrix,
Portland, Ore.

Let the darned thing revolve any way it wants. No true Hi-Fi fan cares about music. It's the sound that's important!
—Ed.

GURGLING SOUND?

Dear Hi-Fi Editor,

I am puzzled. In Erich Blintze's recording of Brahms 1st Symphony, there is a strangle gurgling sound to the trumpets. Is this my set or the recording?

Vladimir Cabot,
Boston, Mass.

It's not your set. This is an example of the new "Seashore Techniques" of Hi-Fi recording where the strings, woodwinds, and percussions play on the beach, and the brass records underwater.—Ed.

TONE-ARM JUMPS?

Dear Hi-Fi Editor,

Whenever I play a certain LP, my tone-arm jumps. Yesterday, it jumped 12 grooves. Is this the record?

Axel O'Toole,
Flagstaff, Ariz.

No, the record for groove jumping is held by a Dauntless H-13-J tone-arm. On December 4, 1956, it jumped 37 grooves on a record played by Clyde Pincus of Yonkers, N.Y. Sorry.—Ed.

RED CARPET DEPT.

Ivan Slobotnavitch, Ace Moscow news correspondent, was recently assigned to photograph and report on the shocking conditions prevalent in this decadent capitalistic country of ours. He arrived here armed with camera, film, pad, and pencil (red), and went straight to work. Fortunately, MAD was able to intercept the dispatch Ivan sent back to *Pravda*. Here, then, is the United States as seen through red-tinted glasses in Ivan's . . .

ЯEPOЯT

"Here is proof that all Americans are warmongers. Even children are armed. For practice, they kill each other!"

"Lynchings are common. Most businesses shut down for the occasion. Not only are the Americans bloodthirsty, they are also illiterate. They can't even spell 'lynch'!"

"With mine own eyes, I have seen long breadlines in the United States!"

*JACK WEBB will return a Julie London album.

TO RUSSIA

PICTURES BY WALLACE WOOD

"Daily, screaming U.S. slave laborers are forced into steel boxcars by uniformed Fascistic guards!"

"U.S. automobiles are poorly made. I have seen the tops of some come off by the mere touch of a finger."

"Clothing is scarce in the United States. Many garments are put on the market only partly completed."

"Most Americans are starving. Newspapers and magazines publish lists of the meager foods the people are permitted to eat!"

"In fact, hunger is so prevalent here, people have taken to eating domestic animals!"

"Lighting facilities in the U.S. are primitive. I have seen Americans reading by the light of 150-year-old kerosene oil lamps!"

"Other, more impoverished people have to be content to eat their meager meals by candlelight!"

I have seen an entire theatre illuminated by only one candelabra!

"Here is proof that Capitalistic bankers bleed the people dry!"

"Americans are so regimented, they are permitted to display their emotions only at given signals!"

"Children are forcefully separated from parents at an early age, and sent off to labor camps!"

"U.S. housewives are forced to operate machines in their own homes!"

"Sanitation facilities are a disgrace. Americans must dump their trash out of windows into streets!"

**PERRY COMO will return a bottle of tranquilizing pills

SICK, SICK, SICK DEPT.

This age we live in has been termed by many as "The Age of Anxiety". And we agree. Today, you have to be a little neurotic, or people look at you like you're not normal. Seems that nowadays, if you don't hate your father, you just don't "belong". And so that readers of MAD shouldn't

HOW NEUROTIC

DO LITTLE EVERYDAY THINGS UPSET YOU?
Yes ☐   No ☐

ARE YOU AFRAID OF MEETING NEW PEOPLE?
Yes ☐   No ☐

ARE YOU THE TYPE WHO WORRIES NEEDLESSLY?
Yes ☐   No ☐

DO YOU OFTEN FEEL THAT LOVED ONES REJECT YOU?
Yes ☐   No ☐

ARE YOU UNNECESSARILY SUSPICIOUS OF EVERYONE?
Yes ☐   No ☐

DO YOU ALWAYS LOOK FOR SYMPATHY FROM OTHERS?
Yes ☐   No ☐

DO YOU HAVE DIFFICULTY MAKING QUICK DECISIONS?
Yes ☐   No ☐   Maybe ☐

ARE YOU ALWAYS TRYING TO ATTRACT ATTENTION?
Yes ☐   No ☐

DO YOU COMPLAIN ABOUT EVERY ACHE AND PAIN?
Yes ☐   No ☐   Oy-vay! ☐

PICTURES BY GEORGE WOODBRIDGE

miss out on this modern way to be interesting and sophisticated, we have prepared the following psychological test which asks the question:

ARE YOU?

CAN YOU ADJUST TO NEW SITUATIONS THAT ARISE?
Yes ☐   No ☐

ARE YOU INTOLERANT OF OTHER PEOPLE?
Yes ☐   No ☐

DO YOU ALLOW OTHERS TO DOMINATE OVER YOU?
Yes Sir ☐   No Sir ☐

DO YOU OFTEN FEEL UNLOVED AND UNWANTED?
Yes ☐   No ☐

DO YOU ONLY SEE THE GLOOMY SIDE OF THINGS?
Yes ☐   No ☐

DO YOU GET STRANGE COMPULSIVE DESIRES OFTEN?
Yes ☐   No ☐

SCORING

**Add 5 for every "Yes" answer.
Subtract 3 for every "No" answer.**

UNDER ZERO

A score below zero shows that you are a typically old-fashioned, emotionally mature-type clod. So, you had better straighten yourself out, or you will wake up one morning so fully adjusted you'll be the laughing stock of your whole neighborhood. Now is the time to get out of your healthy rut and start getting some real anxieties and fears of your very own. Only in this way will you be able to take your rightful place in this sick, sick world of ours.

ZERO TO 50

A score between zero and 50 indicates that you have already started to develop a wholesome-type neurosis, but that there are still some deep-rooted healthy desires in your subconscious which are holding you back from realizing your full neurotic potential. We would suggest that you immediately begin to fight off this inner drive by practicing some time-tested hostile habits. For example, you can start by doubting everything. Then you can become suspicious of your neighbor. Get a little anti-social. Crack up once in a while. Running amok in a Public Library works wonders for beginners.

50 TO 75

A score between 50 and 75 shows that you are a fully-developed MAD-type neurotic, which makes you interesting and sophisticated. Such a guy, we like.

OVER 80

A score of over 80 shows that you are definitely psychotic. It also shows that you suffer from schizophrenia. It also shows that you have paranoiac delusions of grandeur. But mainly, it shows that you can't even add right—because the score only goes up to 75.

**Egocentric... a person who believes he is everything you know you are.

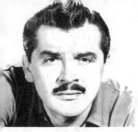

ERNIE KOVACS DEPT. PART I

Strangely Believe It!

PICTURES BY WALLACE WOOD

CONTRARY TO POPULAR OPINION, **WAVING A RED FLAG** AT A **BULL** DOES **NOT** IRRITATE HIM! ACTUALLY **COWS** ARE THE ONES WHO GET IRRITATED WHEN A RED FLAG IS WAVED AT THEM.

The reason a BULL gets mad when a RED FLAG is waved at him is because he dislikes being mistaken for a COW.

ARMAND K. FRECHETTE A FUR TRAPPER from GRANDEBOUCHE, CANADA, TRAPPED A **SINGLE MINK** WORTH **$8000.00** IT WAS DRAPED OVER THE BACK OF A CHAIR AT THE STORK CLUB.

Although a pound of **SALAMI** and a pound of **LIVERWURST** weigh **EXACTLY THE SAME**, THREE POUNDS of **CHOPPED LIVER** weighs more than both put together.

ARTHUR K. LIMBISH a little known **COMEDY WRITER** MEMORIZED THE TAG LINES FOR OVER **930,000** JOKES THE REASON ARTHUR IS A LITTLE KNOWN COMEDY WRITER IS HE NEVER LEARNED THE SET-UP LINES.

THE FANTASTIC ODDS OF **10,000 TO ONE** WERE LEVELED AGAINST "**FIREBRAND**" WINNING THE EPSOM DOWNS DERBY STEEPLECHASE IN 1938

"FIREBRAND" WAS A GARTER SNAKE.

ALTHOUGH THE **MOON** IS ONLY ONE **49TH** THE SIZE OF THE **EARTH**, IT IS **FURTHER AWAY!**

A MAN TRAVELLING ON FOOT FROM **TOKYO,** JAPAN, TO **SAN DIEGO,** CALIFORNIA ...WILL DROWN BEFORE HE GOES A HUNDRED MILES!

**Pioneer... early American who was lucky enough to find his way out of the woods.

THE HOUSE THAT JERK BUILT DEPT.

Here's MAD's version of magazines that urge you to outdo neighbors. Trouble is, it gets messy. Because neighbors also read magazines like

PICTURES BY WALLACE WOOD   CONTINUED ON NEXT PAGE

We converted our patio into a backyard

BEFORE: Patio was an eyesore and a catch-all as well for all the neighborhood fanciers of barbecue and free beer. The Burnstores decided to do something about it.

By Durwood "Greasy" Burnstore

I was busily transplanting snapdragon shoots one afternoon last summer when my wife, Boodie, turned to me and said, "Hey, Meat Head! Whudda we need this patio for? I mean—you know—what's with a patio, anyway? Am I right—or am I wrong? Whaddya say, Meat Head?"

Boodie, of course, had been drinking again. Nevertheless, the idea began to toss itself around in my mind. Other people in our neighborhood had backyards. Maybe we could have one too—with some "do-it-yourself" effort on my part. The more I thought of the idea, the more I liked it. No more smelly barbecues; no more playing host at dull outdoor parties; no more worries about Boodie falling down and hitting her head on the bricks when she was drunk—which was most of the time these days.

The first thing I did was to purchase some dynamite,

(Continued on page 578)

Despite the opposition of free-loading neighbors, Burnstores undertook the arduous task of converting useless patio into a backyard.

AFTER: Months of evening and week-end work paid off as the area miraculously became a backyard. Explained Mr. Burnstore, "It was worth all the time and trouble." Added Mrs. Burnstore, "That's right! *Urrrp!*"

Neighbors still make infrequent attempts to hold barbecues in the Burnstore backyard, but now are kept at bay by rats and other such pests that infest the area. Burnstores plan to add a mosquito breeder next summer.

Tear out that extra downstairs bathroom!

Simple remodeling gave home more storage space—and cut water bills in half, by making frequent baths impractical for this family of fourteen

When the Emil Deifendorfers bought their new home just outside of Wretched, Indiana, two years ago, it seemed to fill all the needs of a family of fourteen—except that it had two bathrooms!

"It was like a nightmare," Deifendorfer recalls now. "I could never remember which bathroom I'd left the glass with my teeth in. And our water bill sky-rocketed as our twelve children capitalized on the extra plumbing facilities to take two, or even three baths a week."

A handyman as well as an efficient home manager, Deifendorfer set to work tearing out downstairs bathroom and converting it into much more needed storage space. With the plumbing now removed, he uses the 7 x 9 room as a convenient spot for storing old magazines and used razor blades. Meanwhile, the family thinks twice before getting into line to use the single remaining bathroom upstairs.

BEFORE: There's valuable space going to waste here. Modern fixtures and glass paneling clutter up room and prevent its use as a closet. Convenient location and facilities offer open invitation to squander expensive water.

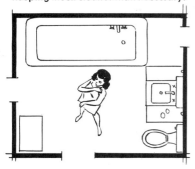

BEFORE: Tools for wasteful indulgent living were all here. Inevitable results were that family did without a much needed storage space while keeping much cleaner than necessary.

AFTER: This is the same room with emphasis now on utility rather than needless luxury. Problem of keeping tile floor clean is solved by making it inaccessible. Deifendorfer did all work himself, but inspiration came from similar room in Langley Collier mansion.

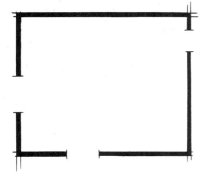

AFTER: Full advantage is taken of available space. Plumbing has been removed and pipes capped to prevent flooding. Ample floor space and high ceilings permit storage of old Life magazines, some dating back to 1936.

Convert your spare bedroom into a basement

By Ozgood Z'Beard

WORK SPACE: One corner of the newly constructed basement is utilized as laboratory where Doctor can perform experiments that time and space limitations do not permit in his office.

More bedrooms than people to fill them in your house? That was the problem facing Dr. Whitney Pfluger only six short months ago.

"When we bought the house," explains Dr. Pfluger, of Monotony, Oklahoma, "I could have sworn we had five children. Imagine my surprise when we moved in and I discovered we only had four. Naturally, it created a spare bedroom problem that we solved with a lot of hard work and almost total lack of know-how."

Using only such basic tools as an axe, a crowbar and a blow-torch, Dr. Pfluger tore out all electric wiring, bricked up walls, covered hardwood oak floors with cement, and ripped off ceilings to expose beams.

The project was so successful that Dr. Pfluger is now hard at work on plans to convert his downstairs knotty pine recreation room into an attic.

PRIVACY: Dr. Pfluger finds that his new basement provides an ideal spot for getting away from the rest of his family and pursuing his many hobbies.

CONVENIENCE: Ample storage space in basement permits the Doctor to save items he has no immediate use for, but that he doesn't want to throw away.

VERSATILITY: Basement also may be used as exercise and game room. Dr. Pfluger keeps in shape by working out here before making his morning house calls.

RECREATION: The newly constructed basement is far enough away from the rest of the house to permit the Doctor to entertain his friends without annoying other members of the family . . . or the police.

They built their house on a lot
22 INCHES WIDE

Wheelwright home is mistaken by many casual observers for lighthouse with no light. Unique dwelling has earned for imaginative and plucky owners a wide reputation as "Those crazy idiots!"

Imagine the surprise of Ewald C. Wheelwright, of Downpour, Iowa, when he received the deed to the property he had craftily purchased at a Sheriff's auction, and discovered that the 800 square feet of land he'd bought was actually a lot 419 feet long and 22 inches wide located between two office buildings in downtown Downpour.

Creative as well as blundering, Wheelwright began work on plans for construction of a home on his uniquely shaped lot. The results, as pictured on this page, have the townspeople of Downpour talking... mostly about other subjects.

The Wheelwrights, who have grown accustomed to moving sideways in their unusual home, acknowledge one serious oversight in the architectural plans.

Says Mrs. Wheelwright, who has been voted out of the Eastern Star since the home was completed, "When you have a house with rooms lined up one behind the other, you should never put a bathroom in the middle as we foolishly did. Whenever somebody takes a bath, the only way other members of the family can get from one part of the house to another is to go out the front door, around the block, and in the back."

The Wheelwrights also find that their new home has spurred them into making a new host of friends, all tall and thin.

Wheelwrights designed home themselves after architect originally assigned job gave up with an acute case of claustrophobia.

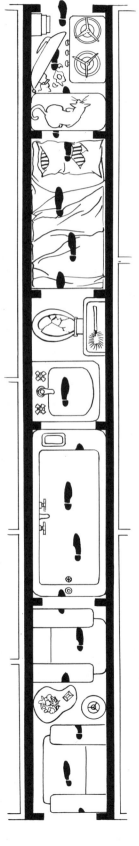

HOW-THE...
for the handyman

Immense savings on water bills, plus elimination of lawn sprinkling results from this unique idea. Using ordinary tools and casters from discarded bed or dresser, merely place lawn on wheels. drag to nearby spot where it's raining.
Hiram Pitnik
Drizzle, Nebr.

Gimletting the auger is easily squared and trued by cross-cutting ten penny 3/16" Stilson and japanning the wing-nut with a two-by-four, slotting the template as shown in the illustration.
Buford Sternwallow
Shrdlu, Minn.

No need to discard chairs with uneven legs. Easy solution for handyman is to place them in room with uneven floors.
Roger Schmeer
Unbalanced, R. I.

This simple expedient ends all danger of hitting ears with claw end of hammer on upswing. Ordinary household adhesive or friction tape keeps ears out of way, and leaves way clear for hitting finger with business end of hammer on downswing.
Alfred E. Neuman
Whatmeworry, Mad.

BIG BROTHER IS MOTIVATING YOU DEPT.

Whether it's magazines, TV, billboards, or even MAD T-shirts, wherever we look these days there's an advertisement. Up to now, we've had the prerogative of reading these ads if we so desired. But now, Madison Avenue has come up with a new advertising technique... officially known as subliminal projection. *We* call it

SNEAKY

HOW IT WORKS...

What happens is, you're sitting in a theater, watching this movie, when...

Suddenly, an advertisement is flashed on the screen for 1/3000 of a second.

This message is flashed so fast, you are not even consciously aware of it.

HOW IT CAN BE USED...

Think of the potential uses for this kind of sneaky advertising. Like for instance, in political campaigns...

Or like if the Movie Industry wanted to eliminate competition by dealing a death-blow to the Television Industry.

Unless the Television Industry wanted to render that possible use harmless by making sure few people ever see it.

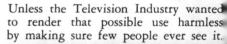

**Friendly Persuasion—THE DALE CARNEGIE INSTITUTE

ADVERTISEMENTS

PICTURES BY BOB CLARKE

But... *hoo-hah!* Your unconscious mind is plenty aware! It read the message!

And now, you suddenly have an amazing craving to drink a bottle of "Coke"!

This is amazing mainly because all of your life you've always hated "Coke"!

Then there's always the use special-interest groups could make of sneaky advertising on signs we *must* look at.

The Army could solve one of its big problems and keep the GI morale high by strategically placed suggestions.

And best of all, some sneaky ads here and there, and people could be influenced into reading good books again.

TO BLAZES WITH THE TRAIL DEPT.

WOOD

A GUIDE TO DANGERS HUNTERS

Every year, thousands of hunters fall sick (and even die) because they enter our forests and wooded areas without any knowledge of the dangers that lie at every turn. Often, perfectly innocent-looking plants, animals and insects may

POISONOUS PLANTS

MOCK POISON IVY

Mock Poison Ivy and Real Poison Ivy are alike in appearance but not in their effect. To test for Mock Poison Ivy, rub it on an unimportant part of your body. If painful swelling occurs almost immediately, then it is indeed Mock Poison Ivy, as swelling from Real Poison Ivy takes much longer. Follow treatment suggested in most First-Aid books for Real Poison Ivy, although it has been proven ineffective in the majority of cases.

**The best things in life are taxable.

Ordinary Poison Ivy

Mock Poison Ivy

PICTURES BY GEORGE WOODBRIDGE

THE VINY POISON QUILLSNAPPER

The Viny Poison Quillsnapper is generally very hard to see, and even harder to find. It winds itself high among the branches of trees in thickly-forested areas. To locate this dangerous vine, simply fashion a long stick and poke it high into the dark foliage overhead. If the pesky plant is there, it will suddenly send down a shower of needle-like quills. As the poison from these quills is usually fatal, once you locate the Viny Quillsnapper, it would be wise not to make camp beneath it, but look for a clearing or open field elsewhere, as any undue prodding is enough to cause it to release its quills.

Poison Quillsnapper
(before prodding)

Poison Quillsnapper
(after prodding)

LORE

SHOULD AVOID IN THE FORESTS

actually carry deadly venom for the unwary. With Fall coming on, as a public service, MAD now offers this illustrated guide to some of the more common dangers found in our forests, so hunters may easily recognize and avoid them.

DANGEROUS ANIMALS

THE FRIENDLY PIRANHAMOUSE

This tiny animal looks just like an ordinary fieldmouse. To identify him, you must first catch him, which is not easy. Once caught, his armpits will reveal two red beautymarks. Extreme caution should be taken not to harm (or even offend) the Friendly Piranhamouse. Angered, he becomes a ferocious maneater whose distress call summons an army of his colleagues. Such an army has been known to strip a human body in less than 12 seconds.

Ordinary Fieldmouse

Friendly Piranhamouse

**A rolling stone gathers momentum.

THE DORMANT ROCKADILLO

Truly Nature's finest camouflage job, the Dormant Rockadillo derives its name from the Armadillo family it belongs to, and the rock-like shell it wears. Many people have come dangerously close to Rockadillos without knowing it. If you suspect a rock of being one, simply lift it up and look on the underside. If you find four tiny feet and a curled up tail, with a swiftly-snapping head, you've got a real one! To remove, build a small fire and heat him up till he releases his grip. The reason he is called "Dormant" is because he sleeps constantly, and only awakens to strike when he has been disturbed.

Ordinary Rock

Dormant Rockadillo

VENOMOUS INSECTS

THE GRAY POISON-SPIT SPIDER

This otherwise ordinary looking spider is an extremely dangerous pest. The only way you can tell him from the thousand or so common spiders is to flip the little devil over on his back for a look at his belly-button. If the belly-button is a bright orange, you can be sure it's a Gray Poison-Spitter. But be careful! This eight-legged demon only spits poison when he is flipped over on his back.

Common Spider   **Poison Spit-Spider**

THE VENOMOUS STING-FLY

There are two major differences between the common House Fly, and the Venomous Sting-Fly. One: The Sting-Fly is very easy to catch, while the House Fly is not. And two: The Sting-Fly bites when caught, while the House Fly does not. The bite causes instant paralysis, which subsides in about 48 hours, after which full recovery follows, with only occasional attacks of nausea and high fever.

Common House Fly   **Venomous Sting-Fly**

HOWEVER, THE GREATEST DANGER TO HUNTERS IN OUR FOREST AREAS IS STILL...

...OTHER HUNTERS!

Volatilis helps Yul Brynner in movies too, as bald head artistically reflects studio lights.°

New painless way to lose your hair in one day

"I used everything trying to break in on Broadway," says Academy Award-winner Yul Brynner, "until I was ready to tear my hair out. Then I tried Volatilis with V-17. And that tore out my hair *for* me. You know the rest of the story. Volatilis started me on the road toward winning The Oscar . . . and incidentally made me *look* exactly like it! So next time you're ready to tear your hair out, try Volatilis with V-17. It does the job *for you!*"

It's that simple. Volatilis makes dry unruly hair easy to manage by getting rid of the stuff altogether! Yet you never have that angry-red, billiard-ball look, because Volatilis combines ground Axolotls and Gasoline with V-17, the new *painless* hair-removing discovery.

Try Volatilis with V-17 today. You'll blow your top!

°*He's under contract to Brunswick-Balke-Collender Co.*

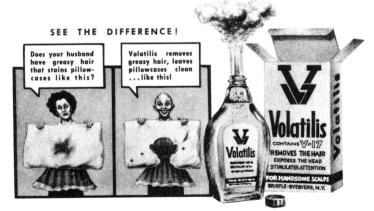

New VOLATILIS Hair Remover with V-17
ANOTHER FINE PRODUCT OF BRISTLE-BYEBYERS

"*I never carry more than $50 in cash,*"

says BRIGITTE BARDOT

"In fact, I never carry *any* cash... mainly because I don't need to!"

"*When I travel, I never need money because everything is paid for by American Expense Account Cheques. And I find these Americans with expense accounts anywhere in Europe, just eager to pad them by taking a girl like me out and paying for little things like my hotel, fur and jewelry bills!*"

AMERICAN EXPENSE ACCOUNT CHEQUES

NEVER CARRY ANY CASH, GIRLS! WHAT CAN YOU LOSE?

THROW THE BOOK AT 'EM DEPT.

With school teachers and parents showing increased alarm over "Why Johnny Can't Read", MAD decided to assign its Educational Research Council to make a study of this pressing problem. The Council reports back that Johnny can't read because (1) he's a clod, and (2) he just can't get interested in the old fashioned primers still in use in most schools. We'd be crazy to solve the former, 'cause then nobody would buy MAD. But we can take care of the latter by replacing old-fashioned dull primers with up-to-date editions of...

THE MAD PRIMER

PICTURES BY JOE ORLANDO

MY FIRST READER
Easy Little Steps for Muddy Little Feet

by Altgeld, Pfeffernick, Cowznofski, Warmerdam, and Umphlott

Lesson 1.

I am Irving
I have a dog.
His name is Schlep.
I teach Schlep to bite the postman.
I do not like the postman because he brings bills and my daddy's draft notices.
The postman does not like me because I am nasty.
Schlep and I like each other.
That figures.

Lesson 2.

I am still Irving.
Sometimes I go to grandpa's farm.
Grandpa's name is Farmer Brown.
He is not really a farmer.
He runs a hot car ring.
Sometimes grandpa lets me put phony license plates on the hot cars.
I like to go see grandpa.
The police would like to see grandpa, too.

Lesson 3.

Irving again.
I am in the first grade.
My teacher is Miss Furd.
I tell the school board Miss Furd is a Commie.
The school board investigates Miss Furd.
Miss Furd is through in this town.

Lesson 4.

I am Sadie.
I am Irving's sister.
This is not the best thing in the world to be.
I have a kitty.
Her name is Fred.
I want to be a nurse someday.
I perform medical experiments on Fred.
Fred lies very still after the experiments.
Rest in peace, Fred.

Lesson 5.

Yoo hoo already.
It's me again—Sadie.
Irving and I have many toys to play with.
Our mother gets them for us at the store.
Our mother is a klepto.
We like the toys she brings us.
Sometimes I let Irving play with my toys.
Sometimes Irving lets me play with his toys.
Big deal.

Lesson 6.

Our daddy works downtown.
He works in a big office building.
He wheels and deals.
Sometimes he writes company checks to pay off his bookie.
Some day the auditors will come.
Bye-bye, Daddy.

Lesson 7.

This is Bobby Smith.
He is our playmate.
Bobby sells reefers to the other children at school.
Sometimes we buy a stick from Bobby.
We light up behind the garage.
Crazy, man.

Lesson 8.

This is Mr. Johnson.
He runs the store in our neighborhood.
He sells meat, vegetables and fruit.
Sometimes while he is selling these things, we sneak in and steal candy.
Sometimes Mr. Johnson catches us.
He says we are no better than common criminals.
We will fix his wagon on Halloween.

Lesson 9.

Hello again already. Sadie speaking.
Irving and I like to go to the zoo.
One day our daddy took us to see the animals.
Irving crawled into the lion's cage.
I asked my daddy to save Irving.
My daddy just smiled and took me home.
Irving came home later.
Tough luck.

Lesson 10.

Irving here.
It is Christmas Day at our house.
Santa Claus brought me a bicycle, blocks, a cowboy suit, an electric train and mittens.
Santa Claus brought Sadie a new doll, a party dress, a coloring book and mittens.
We think Santa Claus is a fink.
I mean what's this with the mittens?

E BEFORE I EXCEPT AFTER Q DEPT.

Our Continuety Editor, who also proofreeds the magazine becawse of his ecstensive knowlege of spelling, has maid the obsivation

PICTURES BY GEORGE WOODBRIDGE

not-so-far-from-wrong

"...and all the old FATERNITY alumni were there."

"I took my boss to dinner and a show RESENTLY."

"...the Congressman introduced a TARRIFIC idea."

"He UPPRAISED the ring for my insurance policy."

"...since he was always a HYPOSENSITIVE person."

"...when he whistled, she gave a CURSERY glance."

**Music Teachers went to Fort Tissimo

that some of the misteaks he comes accross reed better then if they were corect. For instence, take a look at the foulowing...

SPELLING ERRORS

"...explaining why Greek Dramas are so EXITING."

"...the G.I. was then EXCUSSED by the sergeant."

"...when the clerk was APPLING for a better job."

"A hard worker, John was certainly TRUSSWORTHY."

"She is always boasting about her happy MARRAGE,

...and her husband agrees that it's WOUNDERFUL."

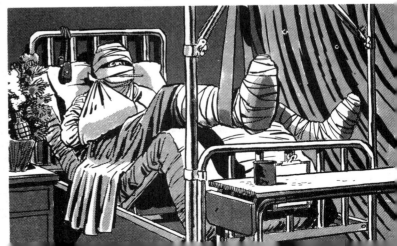

VERSE OF THE PEOPLE DEPT.

Surprising as it may seem, the United States is turning out more brilliant new poets today than ever before. But because so few magazines publish serious poetry, many of these talented young writers remain undiscovered.

With this article, MAD does its bit for the literary upsurge in America by opening its pages to some of the better young poets of today. So prepare yourself to be uplifted by . . .

THE MAD TREASURY OF UNKNOWN POETRY

HIYA, WATHA
by William Worthless Shortfellow

In the bar called Gitchy Goomy
    Where they serve the giggle water,
Way up town on Eighty-second,
    Near the Restaurant Nokomis,
Up by Feldman's Bagel Fact'ry,
    There the shoe clerk, Melvin Watha,
Guzzles cola laced with bourbon;
    Gets ideas then of much grandeur,
Thinks he owns a pipestone quarry;
    Says he's Wally Cox, the mighty;
Pounds the bar and giggles silly,
    Keeps on boozing, gets more sullen,
Doesn't pay the least attention
    When the far more cheery drunkards
Call out gaily, "Hiya, Watha!"
    Downs a shot and then another;
Laps it up till eyes get bleary;
    Falls across the bar unconscious.

PICTURES BY JOE ORLANDO

I WANDERED LONELY AS A CLOD
by William Wordswords

I wandered lonely as a clod
Just picking up old rags and bottles,
When onward on my way I plod,
I saw a host of axolotls;
Beside the lake, beneath the trees,
A sight to make a man's blood freeze.

Some had handles, some were plain;
They came in blue, red, pink, and green.
A few were orange in the main;
The damndest sight I've ever seen.
The females gave a sprightly glance;
The male ones all wore knee-length pants.

Now oft, when on the couch I lie,
The doctor asks me what I see.
They flash upon my inward eye
And make me laugh in fiendish glee.
I find my solace then in bottles,
And I forget them axolotls.

GARBAGE FEVER
by John Leftfield

I must go down to the city dump,
    to the lonely dump and the sky,
And all I ask is a garbage truck
    and a star to steer her by;
And the coffee grounds and the apple peels
    and the rancid fat shaking,
And the grey smoke from the burning trash
    and the grey dawn breaking.

I must go down to the city dump,
    for the call of an old shoe fried
Is a wild call and a clear call
    that cannot be denied;
And all I ask is a windless day
    when the acrid smoke hides the sun,
And the garbage burns in a greasy mess,
    and a thousand rats all run.

I must go down to the city dump,
    to the vagrant gipsy life,
To a mountainous pile of orange peels,
    far away from the city strife;
And all I ask is a merry yarn
    from a laughing dump prospector,
And the quiet sleep and the sweet dream
    of the happy trash collector.

**A fool and his money publish MAD.

IRVING KAHN
by Samuel Tailor Coolman

In Levittown did Irving Kahn
A lovely Cape Cod house decree:
Where Alf, the sacred Neuman, dwelt,
And Nick Fazool and Olaf Svelt,
And even Sean McGee.

There, fifty feet of crab grass ground
With picket fence were girdled round.
A place for little Milt to play,
A port for Irving's Chevrolet.

But just one thing is not the very best:
You can't tell Irving's place from all the rest!

ECHHHVILLE
by Carl Sandhog

Odds maker of the World,
Draft Dodger, Eater of Blintz,
Rider of Railroads and the Nation's Fly Swatter;
Sullen, gassy, sniveling,
City of the Round Shoulders.
They tell me you are awkward, and I believe them; for I have seen your painted women step into open manholes and disappear.
They tell me you are sprawling, and I answer: Yes, it is true; I have seen the real estate promoter build suburbs and go free to build again.
They tell me you are bilious, and my reply is: On your broad boulevards and narrow alleys I have seen men belch.
Come and show me another city with hanging head whining and weak and loathsome and icky.
Backhanded,
Fighting,
Struggling,
Losing,
Dealing, shuffling, redealing.
Proud to be odds maker of the world, draft dodger, eater of blintz, rider of railroads and fly swatter for the nation.

SELECTIONS FROM THE CANTILEVER TALES
by Melvin Chaucer

Whon thot Aprille swithen potrzebie,
The burgid prilly gives one heebie jeebie.
Do pairdish kanzas sittie harrie truman
Though brillig to the schlepper alfred neuman;
And bawthid at the norstrug undeserving,
Do hark the wallish sparkin welcome irving.
It meethid to the mawking swabish crucial,
And battingg forth positionne stanley musial.
Do manny frilling waspish overhearde,
Of bolbing with one slicke chicke, wanda furd.

BEER
by Joyce Killjoy

I think that I shall never hear
A poem lovelier than beer.
The brew that Joe's Bar has on tap,
With golden base and snowy cap.
The foamy stuff I drink all day
Until my mem'ry melts away.
Poems are made by fools, I fear,
But only Schlitz can make a beer.

ON WRITING POETRY THAT ISN'T REALLY POETRY
by Ogden Knish

I've often thought my poems would be neater
If, in addition to rhyming, they had some trace of rhythm; what I mean to say is meter.
But when you're writing for the New Yorker and magazines of that ilk which are read by the pseudo sophisticates, they want you to do it cutely,
And if you send them good old fashioned poetry, they reject it absolutely.

DANNY KAYE DEPT. PART I

In his travels around the world for the United Nations Childrens Fund (UNICEF), for which he serves as Ambassador-at-Large (with Diplomatic Portfolio), Danny Kaye has learned as much about children as any adult has a right to know. And he has found in a col- lection of songs by Milton Schafer, many of the attitudes and m of the amusing foibles of children he has come to know in all la Danny has recorded these songs in a delightfully entertaining alb called "Mommy, Gimme A Drinka Water" (Capitol T-937), in wh

THE NEW

©1957 by Frank Music Corp., 119 W. 57th Street, N.Y.C. Used with permission.

...ccessfully effects a child's voice to express the joy, the ad-
...res, the excitement and the heart-tugs of childhood. And now,
...s "SPECIAL ENGAGEMENT," Danny Kaye performs two of these
...s for MAD readers of all ages. This first one is called...

BABY

**Do unto others before they do unto you.

T'day I wus playin' wit' d' eyes...

An' I stuck my finger in 'er ear...

An' I wuz holdin' her tongue...

PICTURES BY WALLACE WOOD

M-A-A-A-A...

ARE YOU GONNA KEEP DAT NEW BABY?!

THE ROOT OF ALL EVIL DEPT.

Hardly a day goes by that letters don't pour into MAD's palatial tenement offices from deficients all over the country asking: "Just who is this Alfred E. Neuman?" "Where did he come from?" "What does he want?" "Who cares, anyway?" etc. In answer to this great upsurge of interest in the subject, MAD has employed a Geneologist (who works cheap) to investigate Alfred's background and fill us in on

Alfred E. Neuman's FAMILY TREE

PICTURES BY WALLACE WOOD

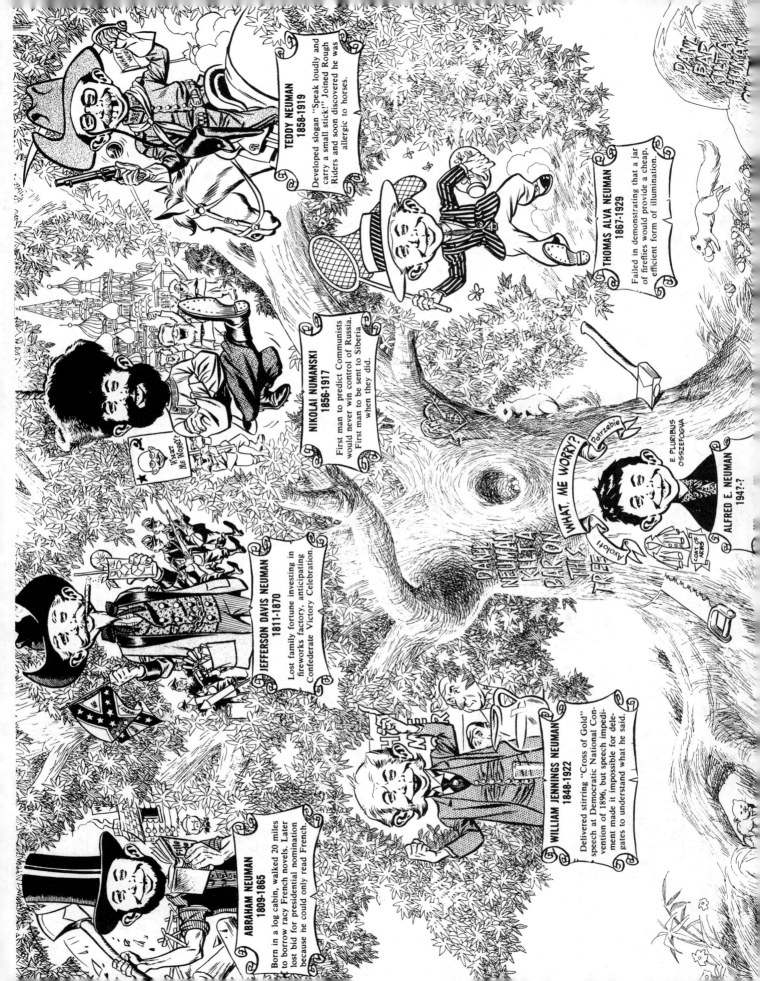

BOB

BOB AND RAY DEPT.

Noting the recent trend on the part of manufacturers to put their new products, no matter what they may be, into Push-Button Pressure Cans, MAD assigned Bob & Ray's ace roving correspondent, Wally Ballew, to investigate the behind-the-scenes story of this new packaging fad. So let's go out to the Blasst Pressure Can Company in Rumney, Vermont, for an educational, on-the-spot interview, as Mr. Ballew presents his

RAY

PRESSURE CAN REPORT

PICTURES BY MORT DRUCKER

**THREE COINS IN THE FOUNTAIN—UNDERWATER

THE SWEET SMELL OF SUCCESS—GONE WITH THE WIND

**SONG OF THE SOUTH—DAMN YANKEES

SID CAESAR DEPT.

Sid Caesar's ten-year television career includes such memorable offerings as "Your Show of Shows", "Caesar's Hour", and "Sid Caesar Invites You." Last summer, Sid and his company appeared in a TV series for the British Broadcasting Company. And this season, Sid has been scoring in a series of critically-acclaimed high-Trendex "Chevy Specials", the first of which won the coveted Sylvania Award for "The Best Comedy-Variety Show" of the year 1958. Sid's well-known comedy characterizations include: *Progress Hornsby*—Jazz Musician, *Somerset Winterset*—Author and World Traveler, and *The Professor*—World's Greatest Authority on the Subject of Everything. And now, Sid Caesar, master satirist in pantomime and monologue, whose appearances make TV-viewing respectable, tries to do the same for MAD...as

MR. SID CAESAR

**THE GREATEST SHOW ON EARTH—THE BIRTH OF A NATION

THE PROFESSOR LECTURES ON SPACE

WRITTEN ESPECIALLY FOR MAD BY SID CAESAR
PICTURES BY WALLACE WOOD

**ANGELS WITH DIRTY FACES—DON'T GO NEAR THE WATER

VIVE LA DIFFERENCE DEPT.

According to Psychologists, most of us clods prefer to follow the "herd instinct" — that is, we prefer to think, look and act alike — which makes us all CONFORMISTS!

Now and then, however, a few clods with imagination break away from the "herd" — and try hard to think, look and act different — which makes them all NON-CONFORMISTS!

Only nowadays, more and more clods are trying to be different, so there are more and more NON-CONFORMISTS! And all these NON-CONFORMISTS are so busy CONFORMING to not being CONFORMISTS, they all wind up CONFORMING to their NON-CONFORMISM!

All except for a small group of bravely idiotic MAD readers — to whom this article is dedicated — mainly because, in this article, we explain in nauseating detail...

HOW TO BE A MAD NON-CONFORMIST

PICTURES BY GEORGE WOODBRIDGE

ONLY MAD NON-CONFORMISTS ACHIEVE GENUINE ORIGINALITY

MUSIC

ORDINARY CONFORMISTS
... play insipid show scores, dismal pop tunes conducted by Jackie Gleason, sickening dance music by Guy Lombardo, rock n' roll hits by Ricky and Elvis, and occasional works of Gershwin and Tchaikovsky on complicated hi-fi sets.

ORDINARY NON-CONFORMISTS
... play obscure folk songs sung by obscure folk, dull chamber music played in dull chambers, Wagnerian operas in their entirety, Gregorian chants, and readings of minor Welsh poets on super-complicated stereo hi-fi sets.

MAD NON-CONFORMISTS
... play bird calls, tap dancing and exercise lessons, transcriptions of Senate Committee hearings, Gallagher & Shean, The Singing Lady, and theme music from famous monster movies on easy-to-operate hand-wound victrolas.

CLOTHING

ORDINARY CONFORMISTS
... wear narrow-shouldered charcoal-grey Ivy League suits, button-down shirts with tight collars, silly caps, cramped Italian style shoes. Females wear Empire dresses and shoes with spike heels that constantly break off.

ORDINARY NON-CONFORMISTS
... wear sloppy-looking sweatshirts, grimy blue jeans, arch-crippling sandals, and scratchy beards. Among the females of this group, leotards are usually substituted for blue jeans, and the scratchy beards are optional.

**A TREE GROWS IN BROOKLYN with THE BAD SEED

MAD NON-CONFORMISTS
... wear smart-looking MAD straight jackets, glamorous opera capes, roomy knickers, comfortable Keds, and lightweight pith helmets which offer good protection in bad weather and provide storage space for day's lichee nuts.

MOVIES

ORDINARY CONFORMISTS
... go in for uninspired Technicolor musicals, stories with happy endings, migraine-provoking Cinemascope, and 6½-hour double features that destroy the eyes, ears, nose, throat and spine.

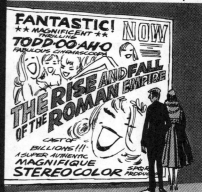

ORDINARY NON-CONFORMISTS
... patronize stuffy out-of-the-way movie houses that show "experimental" films, arty-type films, documentaries, and obscure foreign language pictures with the sub-titles in pidgin Swahili.

MAD NON-CONFORMISTS
... enjoy hand-cranked penny arcade machines which contain film classics like the Dempsey-Firpo fight, Sally Rand's Fan Dance, old Ben Turpin comedies, and Tom Mix pre-adult westerns.

...MONSTRATED BY COMPARING THE HABITS OF ALL THREE GROUPS

READING

ORDINARY CONFORMISTS
... waste their time reading banal best-sellers, trashy whodunits, dull popular magazines, sensational daily newspapers, and commuter time-tables.

ORDINARY NON-CONFORMISTS
... go for childish science fiction novels and scientific magazines, arty paperbacks, boring literary journals, and anthologies of avant-garde poetry.

MAD NON-CONFORMISTS
... read The Roller Derby News, the pre-Civil War Congressional Record, old Tom Swift books, and back copies of Classified Telephone Directories.

PETS

ORDINARY CONFORMISTS
... raise parakeets, cocker spaniels, boxers, collies, turtles, snakes, cats, white mice, parrots and tropical fish.

ORDINARY NON-CONFORMISTS
... raise Russian wolfhounds, French poodles, Weimaraners, ocelots, minks, deodorized skunks and rhesus monkeys.

MAD NON-CONFORMISTS
... raise ant colonies, anteaters, falcons, leeches, octopii, anchovies, water buffaloes and performing fleas.

FOOD

ORDINARY CONFORMISTS
... prefer meals like on menu below.

Sam's chop house
Tomato Juice
Celery and Olives
Vegetable Soup
Sirloin Steak
Green Peas and Carrots
French Fried Potatoes
Hearts of Lettuce Salad
Apple Pie a la Mode
Coffee

ORDINARY NON-CONFORMISTS
... prefer meals like on menu below.

Kerouac's coffee shop
Snails
Sweetbreads
Vichyssoise
Beef Bourguignon
Wild Rice
Pommes de Terre Soufflés
Hearts of Artichoke Salad
Camembert Cheese
Caffé Espresso

MAD NON-CONFORMISTS
... prefer meals like on menu below.

Neuman's way-out house
Hummingbird Tongues on Toast
Kippered Guppy
Purée of Electric Eel
Flamingo Under Glass
Creamed Crab Grass
Sweet Potato Chips
Hearts of Cactus Salad
Licorice Sherbert
Moxie

**MR. BLANDINGS BUILDS HIS DREAM HOUSE with NO DOWN PAYMENT

FAMOUS FUNNIES DEPT.

More and more these days, the trend is toward "realism" in entertainment. Take all them TV heroes, for example. Guys like Bat Masterson, Wyatt Earp, and Jack Benny. These characters aren't made up! No sir! They're taken from real life! If newspaper syndicates were smart, they'd get on the ball, follow the trend, and get more realism in their features by using these...

COMIC STRIP HEROES

(TAKEN FROM REAL LIFE)

PICTURES BY WALLACE WOOD

**Debbie Reynolds in "Since You Went Away"

CONRAD HILTON AND

WERNER VON BRAUN

BRINGING UP BONNIE

HIS HOTELS

—SPACE WIZARD

PRINCE CHARLIE

HYMIE RICKOVER AND HIS ATOMIC SUBS

DICK NIXON IN WASHINGTON

NASSER AND THE ARABS

THE KHRUSHCHEVS

HOFFA THE MENACE

"Kid, what you need is a union! You look like somebody wit' a lot of grievances!"

A SWITCH IN CRIME DEPT.

Every single Saturday night for the past two years on TV, master sleuth and legal eagle, Perry Masonmint, has outwitted District Attorney Hamilton Burgerbits. Now, we don't know if this poor schnook of a DA ever wins any cases during the week, but we certainly think it would be a refreshing change if, just for once, we could turn on our television set, and watch...

THE NIGHT THAT PERRY MASONMINT LOST A CASE

PICTURES BY MORT DRUCKER

We've got this guy Harry Townes **cold,** Burgerbits! He shot a batter at home plate in Yankee Stadium in the third inning of the opening day game! We've got 69,432 witnesses to the murder... the murder weapon... Townes's fingerprints... and a signed confession!

There's just **two** things I want to know, Lieutenant Drag: **When** does he come to trial... and **who's** defending him?

**McCarran-Walters in "Welcome Stranger"

Saturday night! And... Perry Masonmint!

We're **sunk!**

But, Burgerbits! The murder weapon... the seventy-thousand witnesses... the signed confession! I tell you, we've got an **open and shut case** this time!

No, Drag! To Perry Masonmint, that is just **circumstantial evidence!** We need **PROOF!**

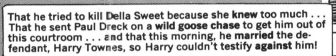

READIN' AND WRITHIN' DEPT.

Some time ago (MAD No. 41), we voiced concern over the dullness of elementary school readers, and presented an up-to-date MAD PRIMER. Now, even the MAD PRIMER is outdated! The single most important thing in the lives of youngsters today is watching "horror movies"! And so, in order to help educate our early grade school kids properly in "horror movie appreciation," we feel schools should offer as required reading...

THE MAD HORROR PRIMER

ART—WALLACE WOOD   STORY—LARRY SIEGEL

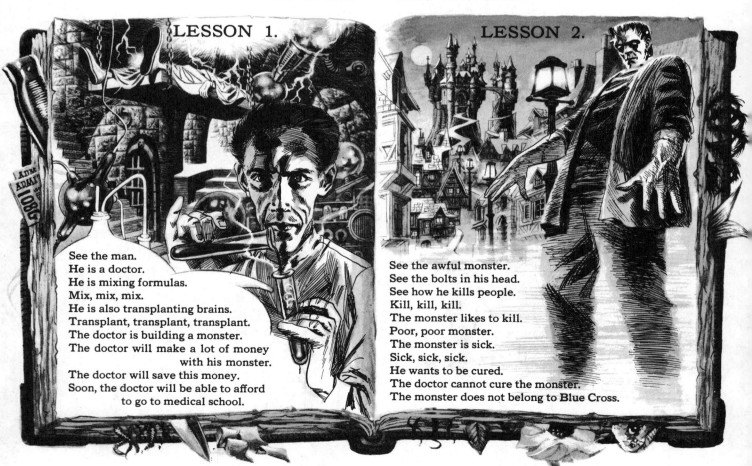

LESSON 1.

See the man.
He is a doctor.
He is mixing formulas.
Mix, mix, mix.
He is also transplanting brains.
Transplant, transplant, transplant.
The doctor is building a monster.
The doctor will make a lot of money with his monster.
The doctor will save this money.
Soon, the doctor will be able to afford to go to medical school.

LESSON 2.

See the awful monster.
See the bolts in his head.
See how he kills people.
Kill, kill, kill.
The monster likes to kill.
Poor, poor monster.
The monster is sick.
Sick, sick, sick.
He wants to be cured.
The doctor cannot cure the monster.
The monster does not belong to Blue Cross.

My First Scary Reader

twisted little thoughts for warped little minds

by five leading experts in Hollywood horror movies.. Karloff, Carradine, Lorre, Chaney and Freed

LESSON 3.

This is a girl.
As if you couldn't tell.
See how her dress is torn.
See how pretty she is.
Pant, pant, pant.
Listen to her scream.
Eeek, eeek, eeek.
The doctor loves the girl.
The monster loves the girl.
The director hates the girl.
She is a terrible actress.
Even the monster is more articulate.

LESSON 4.

See the other girl.
She is a little girl.
She is not so pretty.
Her dress is not torn.
The monster will kidnap the little girl.
She will also scream.
Eeek, eeek, eeek.
She is also a terrible actress.
But she has an excuse.
She is only eight years old.
Then again, she is lucky.
She can always make a living writing horror movies.

**SLEEPING BEAUTY "... rousing and animated!"

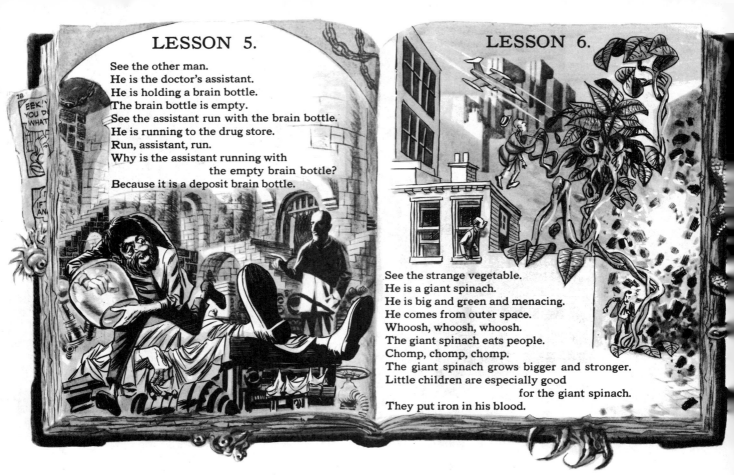

LESSON 5.

See the other man.
He is the doctor's assistant.
He is holding a brain bottle.
The brain bottle is empty.
See the assistant run with the brain bottle.
He is running to the drug store.
Run, assistant, run.
Why is the assistant running with
 the empty brain bottle?
Because it is a deposit brain bottle.

LESSON 6.

See the strange vegetable.
He is a giant spinach.
He is big and green and menacing.
He comes from outer space.
Whoosh, whoosh, whoosh.
The giant spinach eats people.
Chomp, chomp, chomp.
The giant spinach grows bigger and stronger.
Little children are especially good
 for the giant spinach.
They put iron in his blood.

THE BIG COUNTRY "...covers a lot of ground!"

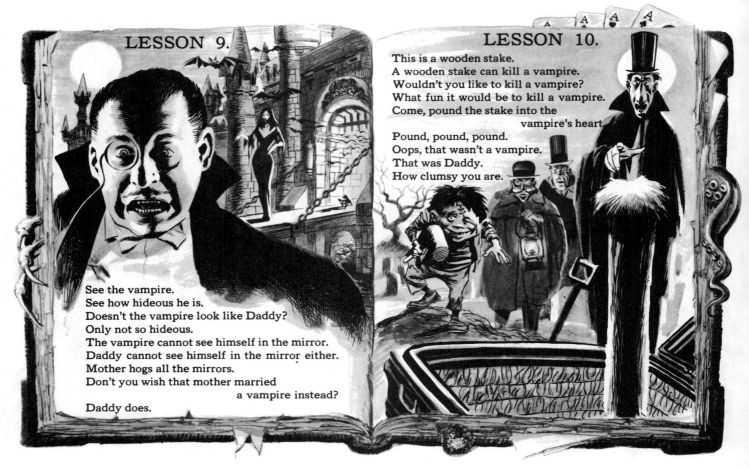

LESSON 9.

See the vampire.
See how hideous he is.
Doesn't the vampire look like Daddy?
Only not so hideous.
The vampire cannot see himself in the mirror.
Daddy cannot see himself in the mirror either.
Mother hogs all the mirrors.
Don't you wish that mother married
 a vampire instead?
Daddy does.

LESSON 10.

This is a wooden stake.
A wooden stake can kill a vampire.
Wouldn't you like to kill a vampire?
What fun it would be to kill a vampire.
Come, pound the stake into the
 vampire's heart.
Pound, pound, pound.
Oops, that wasn't a vampire.
That was Daddy.
How clumsy you are.

LESSON 7.

This is another monster.
He is an ape.
He tears down elevated trains.
Tear, tear, tear.
He tramples people.
Crunch, crunch, crunch.
He is eighty feet high.
He is tall for his age.
That is because he does not drink or smoke.
Don't you wish you did not smoke or drink?

LESSON 8.

This is the Empire State Building.
See the ape climb the Empire State Building.
The ape hates to ride elevators.
Hate, hate, hate.
Soon he will be attacked by planes.
They will be Spads.
and Fokkers.
They will be left over from old
                World War I movies.
But his son will carry on with his work.
Being an ape is more exciting
                than being an accountant.

**THE TEN COMMANDMENTS "... a must!"

LESSON 11.

See the hairy man.
He is a Wolf-Man.
When the moon is full, the Wolf-Man prowls.
Prowl, prowl, prowl.
The Wolf-Man is searching for a victim.
The victim is usually a young starlet.
Woo, woo, woo.
After the day's shooting, the Wolf-Man
      takes off his make-up.
And again he goes searching for
      a young starlet.
Off-screen, the Wolf-Man is still a "Wolf."

LESSON 12.

See the actor struggle.
The Egyptian High Priests are making him
              into a Mummy.
They are wrapping him in bandages.
Wrap, wrap, wrap.
Soon the Mummy is covered from head to
              toe in bandages.
When the scene is over, the Director says, "Cut!"
Cut! Cut! Cut!
But it is too late.
Cutting will do no good.
The actor has suffocated from the bandages.

BERG'S–EYE VIEW DEPT.

The trouble with kids today is: they get the wrong conception of what life's all about. They think life is all play, and the world is just one big playground. We figure they get this idea from the very playgrounds they play in. Because today's playgrounds are built for fun, and they don't prepare kids for the miserable adult life they face. Therefore, we at MAD have designed the following playground equipment to prepare kids for adult life. Mainly, now they can be just as miserable as we adults are, suffering in . . .

MAD THAT PREPARE

THE SHOWY PYRAMID Teaches kids the art of "Social Climbing".

THE SOCIALLY ACCEPTABLE MERRY-GO-ROUND Prepares kids to be good conformists.

THE CONSTANTLY OUT-OF-REACH SWING Teaches kids to face life's frustrations.

So how come I work for MAD?

PLAYGROUNDS

KIDS FOR ADULT LIFE

STORY AND ART—DAVID BERG

THE TANK OF SURVIVAL Teaches kids how to keep their heads above water.

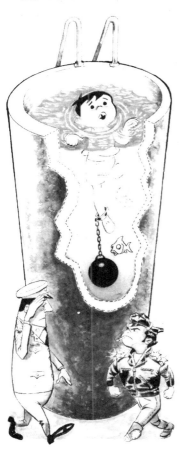

THE LADDERS OF IMPOSSIBILITY Teaches kids how to get along without any visible means of support.

THE BUSINESS TREADMILL Trains kids for the old rat-race.

THE SOCIAL TREADMILL Gets kids into condition for "keeping up with the Joneses".

THE LADDER OF UNREALITY Prepares kids for living way beyond their means.

THE STAIRWAY TO SUCCESS Trains kids to get to the top over the backs of others.

THE SLIDE OF FAILURE Shows kids that the way down is fast and easy.

THE NET OF TRUTH Teaches kids that, though life may look like a bed of roses, it's really full of thorns.

THE STEAMER PLAY HOUSE Prepares kids for today's "Pressure Cooker" society.

THE LIVE-FOR-TODAY SANDBOX Teaches kids to have fun before time runs out.

THE BAR OF MORALITY Trains kids to walk the straight and narrow.

THE RINGS OF INFLATION Teaches kids the art of stretching the dollar.

One kind of husband... <u>two</u> kinds of underwear

Why do you suppose so much Hames underwear for all kinds of husbands is bought by their wives? Because women have an uncanny knack of picking out designs men wouldn't be caught dead in, no less buy themselves! That's why we run these ads which encourage wives to buy their husbands' underwear for them. Mainly, we're trying to get rid of all these shorts with ridiculous designs we're stuck with!

Hames Knitting Co, Wemus-Sellum, N.C.   •   European: Macht Schnell Undzell, Dershtripeses, Germany   •   Russian: Pusha Pohka, Dotz, U.S.S.R.

underwear for men and boys

SPECIAL DELIVERY DEPT.

Whether it's uttered in the parlance of the great "rail-splitter," or in the jargon of the modern "ear-splitter," here's a speech by a man who really knew how to swing his axe. MAD herewith helps to celebrate the Sesquicentennial (whatever in heck that is!) of Abraham Lincoln's birth by offering a "Cool School" version of...

LINCOLN'S GETTYSBURG ADDRESS

THE OLD VERSION

Fourscore and seven years ago our fathers brought forth on this continent a new nation, conceived in Liberty, and dedicated to the proposition that all men are created equal. Now we are engaged in a great civil war, testing whether that nation, or any nation so conceived and so dedicated can long endure. We are met on a great battlefield of that war. We have come to dedicate a portion of that field as a final resting-place for those who here gave their lives that that nation might live. It is altogether fitting and proper that we should do this. But in a larger sense we cannot dedicate, we cannot consecrate, we cannot hallow this ground. The brave men, living and dead, who struggled here, have consecrated it far above our power to add or detract. The world will little note, nor long remember what we say here; but it can never forget what they did here. It is for us, the living, rather to be dedicated here to the unfinished work which they who fought here have thus far so nobly advanced. It is rather for us to be here dedicated to the great task remaining before us, that from those honored dead we take increased devotion to that cause for which they gave the last full measure of devotion; that we here highly resolve that these dead shall not have died in vain; that this nation, under God, shall have a new birth of freedom, and that government of the people, by the people, and for the people, shall not perish from the earth.

THE NEW VERSION

Fourscore and like seven years ago our old daddies came on in this scene with a new group, grooved in free kicks, and hip to the Jazz that all cats make it the same. Now we're real hung up in a crazy big hassle, digging whether that group, or any group so grooved and so hip can keep on swinging. We're making it on a wild spot of that hassle. We've got eyes to tag a little of that spot as a last lay-down pad for those who here conked out so that group might still score. It's frantically cool and jivey that we're on this kick. But in a bigger ribble we can't shake up, we can't sound off, we can't even clue in this jazz. The cool cats, with us and down under, who flipped here, have pegged it straighter than we could ever mess with. The squares will never buy this bit, nor dig the lyrics we spiel here; but they can't ever put down what those studs did here. It's for us, the on-cats, who ought to pick up on those still-wailing blues which the off-cats who goofed here have blown so crazily up till now. Man! Like we really ought to be here with eyes fixed on this wild gig that still needs action, that from those far-out D.O.A.'s we get a little higher on that kick for which they really went and flipped their gaskets; that we take it on to set straight that these cats shall not have kicked off square; that this group under God, shall blow a crazy new sound, and that a hot combo of the hipsters, by the hipsters, and for the hipsters, shall not cut out from this scene.

ART—MORT DRUCKER

POMP-ADORE DEPT.

We've got a confession to make! Confession being: MAD is not the funniest magazine on the newsstands today! There are magazines that are much funnier! Mainly, those serious magazines for "Teenagers"! You'll see what we mean if you study this typical example called...

ART—JOE ORLANDO   STORY—LARRY SIEGEL

**"WHO CARES WHAT PEOPLE SAY—Salvador Dali

"REACHING FOR THE MOON—Wernher Von Braun

TEENAGE MAGAZINE PRESENTS:

Teenager of the Month

15-YEAR-OLD MURRAY BLECH

Once again, TEENAGE Magazine's Ace Photographer, Ninny Sklar, takes you on a pictorial journey through a typical day in the life of a typical teenager. Our typical teenager this month is fifteen-year-old Murray Blech...

UP AT 7:00 A.M., Murray combs his hair until 9:15. Then he combs his sideburns until 11:00. At 11:01, he'll sit down with his guitar and compose his daily Rock 'n Roll song. At 11:08, Murray will record the song on his home recorder. At 11:14, his own record company, *Compost Discs,* will press it, and release it. By noon, it will sell a million copies...

AT 12:15, Murray is out in the backyard, puttering around his real gone custom car until 3:30. You'd never believe it, but that car Murray is standing next to was once a 1960 Cadillac. All the ingenious Murray did was nose it, deck it, lower it 12 inches, and throw away the engine, the brakes, the transmission and the chassis. Then he hitched a pony on the front to pull it. You'd never believe it, but that pony was once a horse. All the ingenious Murray did was nose him, deck him, lower him 12 inches, and throw away some skin, bones and hair. Any of you guys and gals can do the same thing!

AT 4:00 O'CLOCK Murray is at the Bandstand Show (natch), dancing with a real cool chick. He loves the other kids at the show because they're loads of fun, and not the least bit self-conscious about being on TV. Murray hasn't missed one afternoon dancing on The Bandstand Show in two-and-a-half years... an amazing record, considering the Show is in Philadelphia... and Murray lives out in Oregon.

AT 8:00 P.M. Murray and his chick (his steady, natch) attend a triple horror show at the Drive-In. They aren't horrified at any of the feature films. They're horrified at the musical short, in which a Rock 'n Roll singer has accidentally hit a clinker... and pronounced a real understandable English word! After taking his chick home, Murray will return to his own house at 2:00 AM! He will comb his hair and sideburns until 4:00 AM and then retire.

And so ends a busy day in the life of TEENAGE Magazine's "Teenager of the Month," Murray Blech. Of course, tomorrow being Saturday, and no school, he'll be able to relax...

PENMATES

*I'd love to hear from boys 16-19. I'm 15, and have brown hair and blue eyes. I love dancing, Elvis, Ricky, Dick, Sal, Pat, Tommy, Fabian, James Dean, hot rods, short shorts, pop records, stock cars and my mother, in that order.
Phoebe Newt
142 S. Green
Stronghead, Montana

*I'm a cool widow of 14. My late husband and I used to dance on the bandstand show. He was killed while we were fighting nine other couples for a good camera position. I'd sure like to meet another cute guy of 15. But not for another week. After all, how would it look?
Yetta Blintzner
185 Carter St.
Littleliver Pill, North Dakota

*Hi, everybody! I just arrived, and I'm lonesome! I'm 18. I love hot rods. My favorite relaxation is playing "chicken" at 110 MPH. Am anxious to hear from Jimmy Dean and the rest of the wild bunch who made it here before me.
Monty Monroe
Block 4, Row D.
Forest Lawn Cemetery
Los Angeles, California

*I'm 16, 5' 8", 162 lbs., and I have brown wavy hair, green eyes, a sparkling smile, dimples, broad shoulders, a slim waist, and well-muscled arms and legs. Actually, I don't want to meet anybody. I just love to describe myself!
Myron Gorzz
No address given

*Hi, there. I'd like to meet a nice, settled, serious-minded teen-age girl. I have a great sense of humor, and I'm loads of fun at large dinners and funerals.
G. Jessel
Hollywood, California

*I'm a lonely fellow who is quite short. Although I'm 17, I'm only 4' 3" tall. I'd like to meet a nice short chick. Or if not, maybe 53 other guys my height to help me set a new telephone booth-stuffing record.
Steve Vonce
88 Skincondition Street
Noxema, Vermont

**LIPSTICK ON YOUR COLLAR—Helena Rubinstein

Dear Seymour

If you have a question you'd like answered, address a letter to Dear Seymour, *c/o* TEENAGE, *Ira's Candy Store, Palo Alto, Calif. All correspondence will be treated with utmost discretion, but we ask that you include your name and address, your phone number and your picture. All letters become the property of* TEENAGE. *All teenagers become the property of Seymour if he likes your looks.*

Dear Seymour:
 I'm sick and tired of immature teenage boys. I'd like to go out with an older fellow. I was thinking of calling Carl Sandburg for a date next Saturday, and also asking him if he has a friend for my friend. What do you think?
　　　　　　　　　Birdie,
　　　　　　　　Chicago, Ill.

I think you're quite immature, and have a lot to learn about dating, and life in general! Your idea is childish and completely ridiculous! After all, why drag a friend along on a first date?

Dear Seymour:
 I am 13 years old, and have only recently learned about kissing. I must admit that I am a bit confused. For example, is kissing my mother "different" from kissing a date?
　　　　　　　　　Irving
　　　　　　　　Brooklyn, N. Y.

I'm afraid I can't answer that for you, Irving. I've never kissed your mother!

Dear Seymour:
 My wife is a nice average teenage girl, and we have two average teenage children, the older of which is jealous of the younger. Anyway, last month my car was stolen, and ever since it happened, my wife has refused to date me. She insists that no average teenage girl dates a fellow without a car. This is maddening. Please advise.
　　　　　　　　　Bernie
　　　　　　　　Absalom, N. C.

Stop worrying. Show your older child as much love as you show your younger, and he won't be jealous anymore!

Dear Seymour:
 I am 17, very pretty, and come from a good family. Recently I met a fellow who is 19, very handsome, has a car, a good job, and also comes from a good family. We are engaged to be married, and are very happy. What I'd like to know is: how can I have problems like other teenagers?
　　　　　　　　　Muriel
　　　　　　　　Montclair, N. J.

Join clubs, develop new interests, meet new people, and above all . . . be yourself!

Dear Seymour:
 Do you think it's all right for a 15-year old teenage girl to go away for a month with a married man to a cabin in Maine, and go out with him to bars every night?
　　　　　　　　　Goldie
　　　　　　　　St. Louis, Mo.

Yes, providing you're back in the cabin no later than 10:00 P.M. on school nights.

Dear Seymour:
 I have a terrible teenage problem, and if someone doesn't solve it for me, I'll go out of my mind. Here I am, going on 14, and I still haven't written or recorded a single Rock 'n Roll hit song. Is there something terribly wrong with me?
　　　　　　　　　Marvin
　　　　　　　　Sarasota, Fla.

Yes!

Dear Seymour:
 How come you never answer questions with funny jokes, like "Abby" and "Ann" do?
　　　　　　　　　Klaus,
　　　　　　　White Sands, N. M.

How's this? The best way to drive a baby buggy is tickle his feet!

Dear Seymour:
 You call that a funny joke?
　　　　　　　　　Klaus,
　　　　　　　White Sands, N. M.

Why don't you ask funny questions like "Abby" and "Ann's" readers do?

DISKVILLE
LATEST RECORD NEWS
by Sheldon "Groovy" Abisch

♭ ♭ *There's no short cut to fame in pop music!* Take that exciting new vocal group, **THE BARNYARDERS**. These four swinging young plumbers' apprentices from Decatur, Illinois, were singing together for nearly two and a half weeks before they made it!

♯ ♯ *Have you dug the sensaysh new platter,* "The Belly-Roll Rock-a-Billy Boogie Cha Cha Boogie Billy-a-Rock Roll Belly"? Lyrics for this great new tune, in case you don't know, were written by **BING CROSBY'S** new teenage son, **HARRY!** He's 15! Months, that is . . . and a real comer!

♭ ♭ *It looks like that great Rock 'n Roll Singer,* **FABIAN**, will join **KING ELVIS**, **PAT**, **RICKY**, and **SAL** as a movie star. A talent scout from **20th**, heard **FABE's** new smasheroo waxing of "Rockin' at the Taj Mahal", and signed him immediately for a juicy role in the new flick based on the life of **DR. JONAS SALK**. Handsome **FABE** will play a swinging teenage heart specialist. Good luck, **FABE!**

♯ ♯ *Betcha can't guess what R 'n R great* **FRANKIE AVALON** is planning to do with the royalties from his fabulous new disc, "My Teenage Lips Are Chapped From Kissing an Ice Cold Chick"! **FRANKIE's** going to buy the British Isles. Smart move, **FRANKIE!**

♭ ♭ *There's no stopping* **RICKY NELSON** these days. The Dee Jays tell me he now has 43 platters in "The Top Ten"! Good work, **RICK!**

♯ ♯ **RUMORSVILLE:** No matter what you may hear, there is *no truth* to the rumor that **FABIAN** and **LEONARD BERNSTEIN** are feuding! We've also checked the rumor that **THE FLEETWOODS**, **THE BONNEVILLES**, **THE IMPALAS**, **THE CADILLACS**, **THE CORVETTES**, and **THE ELDORADOS** Vocal Groups are backed by General Motors, and it's *definitely not true!* They're backed by Chrysler!

♭ ♭ **PLATTERS TO WATCH** (but not to listen to): "Tired Teenage Feet in Dirty Teenage Sneakers" by **THE SNORERS** on the Swill Label; "The Edward G. Robinson Rock" by **JACK LARUE** on the Flybynight Label; "That Teenage Grandma of Mine" by **NICKY KHRUSHCHEV** on the Red Label; The "Gazzadzt Gdflg Ooh-Ah Mnf Cha Cha Cha" by **THE SPEECH MAJORS** on the Iodine-bottle Label.

♯ ♯ **NEWCOMERS:** Watch for an exciting new song writer named Cole Porter! One of his tunes made the Number 98 spot all over the country this week, despite the fact that it is not R 'n R. And they tell me Cole isn't even a teenager. Which proves that there's truly opportunity for all here in the good ol' rockin' U.S.A.!

How Much Do You Know About KISSING?

by Sonia Schlepp
TEENAGE Magazine's Kissing Editor

How much do you teenage teenagers know about kissing? Sonia Schlepp, our Kissing Editor, has devised this special! quiz so you can find out. Simply answer the following statements **True** *or* **False.** *The correct answer with an explanation follows each statement.*

(1) IT IS BEST TO KISS A GIRL WITH YOUR EYES CLOSED.

False. It is best to kiss a girl with your lips!

(2) YOU CAN LEARN A LOT ABOUT KISSING FROM A GOOD HYGIENE BOOK.

True. But it's not much fun kissing a Hygiene book!

(3) KISSING IN A PARKED CAR CAN GIVE A GIRL A BAD REPUTATION.

True. Unless she's with a boy!

(4) IF YOU TRY TO KISS A GIRL THE FIRST TIME YOU GO OUT WITH HER, SHE WILL LOSE RESPECT FOR YOU, AND SHE WON'T GO OUT WITH YOU AGAIN.

True. Perhaps the following example will illustrate. Several months ago there was a fire in my house. As I dashed into the hall, a fireman appeared, picked me up, and said, "C'mon, Miss, I'll take you out!" We dashed out into the street seconds before the building collapsed. He was so happy we were safe, he tried to kiss me. Since it was the first time he'd taken me out, I naturally turned him down. What's more, I lost respect for him. And he later regretted his action, too. Because every fire after that, I went out with another fireman!

(5) A KISS ON THE HAND MAY BE QUITE CONTINENTAL.

True. But diamonds are a girl's best friend!

(6) THINKING ABOUT KISSING TOO MUCH CAN BE HARMFUL.

True. Let me cite the case of a teen-ager who spent a whole day thinking about kissing. The same evening, he died as a result of severe electrical damage to his brain. He would not have died that evening if he had not thought about kissing all day, and if the Governor's reprieve had arrived at the Death House in time!

(7) TOO MUCH THINKING ABOUT HUGGING CAN BE HARMFUL.

I haven't the slightest idea! I'm TEENAGE Magazine's **Kissing** Editor!

NEW TEENAGE MAGAZINE'S FREE ALL-IN-ONE FAN CLUB

Hey, guys and gals! Tired of joining a hundred different clumsy and involved FAN CLUBS? How about joining **one** single different clumsy and involved FAN CLUB? We're talking about TEENAGE Magazine's NEW **FREE** ALL-IN-ONE FAN CLUB! It's absolutely **FREE,** and it's one of the few really legitimate fan club organizations not run by a fly-by-night company. All you have to do to join is send your name and address to: TEENAGE Magazine's New **FREE** All-In-One Fan Club, c/o Ira's Candy Store, Palo Alto, Calif. Remember, this ALL-IN-ONE FAN CLUB is absolutely **FREE!**

UPON JOINING EVERY MEMBER RECEIVES ABSOLUTELY FREE:

1. A beautiful All-In-One Fan Club Membership Card.

2. 8 Beautiful full-size photos of Elvis, Ricky, Sal, Tab, Fabian, etc.

3. 8 wallet-size photos of Elvis, Ricky, Sal, Tab, Fabian, etc.

4. 8 photo-size shots of the wallets of Elvis, Ricky, Sal, Tab, Fabian, etc.

5. A beautiful candid photo of Elvis, Ricky, Sal, Tab, Fabian, and all the other R 'n R stars in a scene from their new all-in-one movie, "A Hundred Men in Search of a Voice."

6. A gorgeous composite wallet-size blow-up photo of all the members of the families of Elvis, Ricky, Sal, Tab, Fabian, etc., as children.

REGISTRATION FEE (during a solar eclipse, if it should occur on Leap Year Day, and Grand Central Station is empty between the hours of 7:00 AM and Noon)....25¢
ALL OTHER TIMES $175

BONUS: A Beautiful 8 x 10 Glossy Photo of Secretary of Agriculture Ezra Taft Benson as a teenager!

EXTRA BONUS: A beautiful 8 x 10 Glossy Photograph of Bing Crosby's new son, Harry . . . as an adult!

SENSATIONAL EXTRA BONUS: Every reader who joins this fan club, and sends all the money required to: TEENAGE Magazine's New **FREE** All-In-One Fan Club, c/o Ira's Candy Store, Palo Alto, Calif., will receive a beautiful 8 x 10 Glossy Photo of Ira's Candy Store being blown up to make room for the new Freeway, and the editors of this magazine scurrying off to a Brazil-bound plane with sacks of money.

"SOMEBODY LOVES ME, I WONDER WHO—Rafael Trujillo

"Stop pushing — you'll all get a chance to talk to Grandma"

How long has it been since you enjoyed a Long Distance visit?

CELL TELEPHONE SYSTEM Remember... "It's Fun to Phone!"